OCR GCSE

Stephen Lucas
Mark Pedroz
Brian Penman
Helen Rees-Bidder

English Literature

OXFORD
UNIVERSITY PRESS

OXFORD
UNIVERSITY PRESS

Great Clarendon Street, Oxford, OX2 6DP, United Kingdom

Oxford University Press is a department of the University of Oxford. It furthers the University's objective of excellence in research, scholarship, and education by publishing worldwide. Oxford is a registered trade mark of Oxford University Press in the UK and in certain other countries

British Library Cataloguing in Publication Data

Data available

ISBN 978-019-837433-6

10 9 8 7 6 5 4 3 2

Printed in China by Leo Paper Products Ltd.

Contents

OCR GCSE English Literature specification overview

You are studying for a GCSE English Literature qualification from OCR. The OCR GCSE English Literature specification has been designed to help you explore a wide variety of literary texts from across a range of genres and time periods, developing your independent and critical reading skills.

What you will be studying

In preparation for your two GCSE English Literature exams you will be studying the following:

- A modern prose or modern drama text
- A 19th-century novel
- The OCR Poetry Anthology: *Towards a World Unknown*
- Unseen poetry
- A Shakespeare play.

The exam papers

The grade you receive at the end of your OCR GCSE English Literature course is entirely based on your performance in two exam papers. The tables opposite provide a summary of these two exam papers.

Grades

Your GCSE English Literature grade will be awarded solely on the basis of your performance in these two exams and you will be awarded a grade from 1 to 9, with 9 being the top grade.

Exam paper	Reading and Writing questions and marks	Assessment Objectives	Timing	Marks (and % of GCSE)

Paper 1: Exploring modern and literary heritage texts	**Section A: Modern prose or drama**
	Exam text:
	• One modern prose or drama text
	Exam questions and marks:
	• One question with two parts:
	  a) Extract-based question on set text and same-genre unseen extract (20 marks)
	  b) Linked question on the set text only (20 marks)
		A01
		A02
		A03
			2 hours
			Recommended 1 hour 15 mins on Section A and 45 mins on Section B
				Section A: 40 marks
				25% of total GCSE

	Section B: 19th-century prose Exam text: • One 19th-century text Exam questions and marks: • One question on the studied text from a choice of two, one of which will be based on an extract printed on the exam paper (40 marks)	A01 A02 A03 A04		Section B: 40 marks 25% of total GCSE

Exam paper	Reading and Writing questions and marks	Assessment Objectives	Timing	Marks (and % of GCSE)

Paper 2: Exploring Poetry and Shakespeare	**Section A: Poetry across time**
	Exam text:
	• One cluster of poems from the OCR Poetry Anthology plus unseen poetry
	Exam questions and marks:
	• One question with two parts:
	  a) Question on one poem from the studied cluster of the Anthology and an unseen poem on a similar theme (20 marks)
	  b) Linked question on a different studied poem of your choice from the Anthology (20 marks)
		A01
		A02
			2 hours
			Recommended 1 hour 15 mins on Section A and 45 mins on Section B
				Section A: 40 marks
				25% of total GCSE

	Section B: Shakespeare Exam text: • One Shakespeare play Exam questions and marks: • One question on the studied play from a choice of two, one of which will be based on an extract printed on the exam paper (40 marks)	A01 A02 A03 A04		Section B: 40 marks 25% of total GCSE

Introduction to this book

How this book will help you

Develop your knowledge, understanding and appreciation of a range of novels, drama and poetry

The primary aim of this book is to develop and improve your understanding of English Literature. Crucially however, in this book you will be doing this in the context of what the exam papers will be asking of you at the end of your course. So, the skills you will be practising throughout this book are ideal preparation for your two English Literature exam papers.

Explore the texts that you will face in the exams

In your English Literature exams you will have to respond to a number of texts. In order to prepare you fully for the texts that you will face in the exam, this book is structured so you can develop your understanding of the different types of text, novels, plays and poetry, through a range of activities.

Become familiar with the Assessment Objectives and the exam paper requirements

Assessment Objectives are the skills that underpin all qualifications. Your GCSE English Literature exam papers are testing four Assessment Objectives. This book develops the necessary skills, in the context of these Assessment Objectives.

The Assessment Objectives for GCSE English Literature are as follows:

The Assessment Objectives	
AO1	Read, understand and respond to texts. Students should be able to: • maintain a critical style and develop an informed personal response • use textual references, including quotations, to support and illustrate interpretations.
AO2	Analyse the language, form and structure used by a writer to create meanings and effects, using relevant subject terminology where appropriate.
AO3	Show understanding of the relationships between texts and the contexts in which they were written.
AO4	Use a range of vocabulary and sentence structures for clarity, purpose and effect, with accurate spelling and punctuation.

> **A note on spelling**
>
> Certain words, for example 'synthesize' and 'organize' have been spelt with 'ize' throughout this book. It is equally acceptable to spell these words and others with 'ise'.

How is this book structured?

This Student Book will be divided into four main chapters that mirror the structure of the exam papers:

- Chapter 1: Modern prose and drama
- Chapter 2: 19th-century prose
- Chapter 3: Poetry
- Chapter 4: Shakespeare

The units within each chapter will develop your understanding of the texts you will meet in that part of the exam. Each chapter opens with two introductory pages that explain the skills you will be focussing on and will link the learning to the exam requirements.

The units all include a range of activities to help you develop your skills in English Literature.

Getting ready for the exam

The final unit in each chapter pulls all of the skills together for that part of the exam paper and provides preparation for the exam. It provides guidance on the question types you will encounter as well as tips for including quotation and textual references and help with timing and planning your responses.

What are the main features in this book?

Activities, Support and Stretch

To develop your reading responses to the range of texts you will be studying for GCSE Literature as well as developing your writing skills, you will find many varied activities. The activities will provide opportunities for you to be involved in collaborative learning, independent research, reflect on your progress, debate and organise your learning and ideas. You will also have opportunities for self and peer review.

The 'Support' feature for some of the activities provides additional help whilst the 'Stretch' feature introduces further challenge to help develop a more advanced response.

Tips, Key terms and glossed words

These features help support your understanding of key terms, concepts and more difficult words within a source text. These therefore enable you to concentrate fully on developing your reading and writing skills.

Progress check

At the end of each chapter you will find regular formative assessment in the form of 'Progress checks'. These enable you to establish, whether through peer or self-assessment, how confident you feel about what you have been learning.

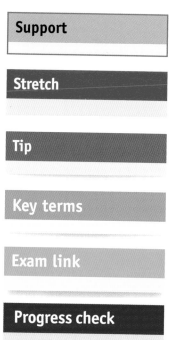

Support

Stretch

Tip

Key terms

Exam link

Progress check

Effective revision

Do not let anyone persuade you that you can't revise for an English Literature exam. As with any subject, careful preparation and revision will improve your chances of getting a good result.

It is really important to have a good knowledge of your modern text, 19th-century novel, poetry cluster and Shakespeare play. To do this, you will need helpful revision notes.

Organizing your notes is the key to success. You can create helpful revision notes, in a variety of ways, listed below. These will be explored in the activities in this book when analysing your set texts and the poems in your cluster:

- Spider diagrams to explore characters, themes, links and relationships.

- Quotation banks to remember quotes to use as evidence in your answers.

- Timelines to explore key events and the chronology in your set texts.

- Lists and brief notes to revise key pieces of information, such as language features.

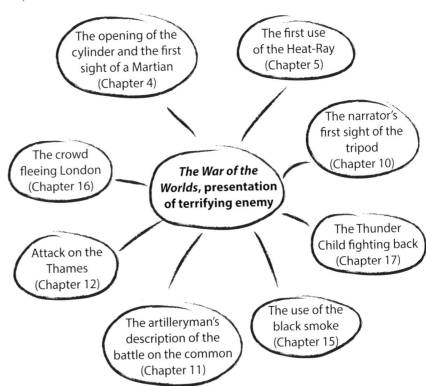

In the weeks leading up to the exam, you should re-organize your notes so that they are useful and can be learned easily. This can be done in different ways to suit your learning style. Some students like to rewrite their notes summarizing the key points; some like to put their notes onto cue cards, or large sheets of paper and stick them on their walls; others like to buy a special revision notebook and re-organize their notes in that.

Whatever you choose, make sure that you are learning enough knowledge that you can use in your exam answers. Remember that you will not have your set texts in the exam with you. When revising, don't learn long quotations. Concentrate instead on short, precise quotations for each character and theme so that you can comment in detail on their language and its effect.

The OCR Poetry Anthology: *Towards a World Unknown*

As part of your GCSE English Literature course you will be studying one of the following themed poetry clusters from the OCR Poetry Anthology, *Towards a World Unknown*:

Love and Relationships

Conflict

Youth and Age

It is important that you know which cluster you are studying and that you read poetry more widely related to your theme. This will help you prepare for the comparison task based on a poem you have studied in the Anthology and the unseen poem.

Further OCR GCSE English resources

OCR GCSE English Language Student Book 1: Developing the skills for Component 01 and Component 02

Student Book 1 includes thematically-focused skills-based units to help develop key reading and writing skills in a motivational context. Structured around the Assessment Objectives, Student Book 1 provides the ideal preparation for students as they embark on this GCSE course.

The themes covered:

- On the mind
- This life
- Friendship and family
- New horizons
- War and conflict
- Reflect and review

OCR GCSE English Language Student Book 2: Assessment Preparation for Component 01 and Component 02

Student Book 2 provides students with all the exam preparation and practice that they need to succeed. The book is divided into Component 01 and Component 02 sections with each component further divided into reading and writing sections to reflect the format of the two exam papers. Within each section, students are guided through the Assessment Objective and question requirements. The book features:

- an overview of what to expect in the exams
- paper by paper and question by question practice
- a range of texts and tasks similar to those students will encounter in the exam
- activities to practise and reinforce the key skills with advice on how to improve their responses
- marked sample student responses at different levels
- opportunities for self-assessment and peer-assessment
- sample exam papers.

OCR GCSE English Language Teacher Companion

The Teacher Companion provides holistic support for teachers to help them plan and deliver their GCSE programme, including:

- specification insight and planning guidance to aid planning and delivery of the specification

- teaching tips and guidance for effective lesson delivery of the material in Student Book 1, with additional support for differentiation and personalisation

- exam preparation guidance and planning with links to OCR English Language Student Book 2

- guidance and support for delivering Spoken Language assessments

- links to, and guidance on, the additional resources on the accompanying OCR GCSE English Language Teacher Companion CD-ROM.

OCR GCSE English Language Teacher Companion CD-ROM

The Teacher Companion is accompanied by a CD-ROM containing the following resources:

- Activity worksheets to support and extend activities in Student Book 1

- Differentiated worksheets to support and stretch activities in Student Book 1

- Progress Check self-assessment and peer-assessment checklists

- Mark schemes for end-of-chapter assessments in Student Book 1

- Mark schemes for sample exam papers in Student Book 1

- Short, medium and long-term editable plans to aid the planning and delivery of the course.

1 Modern Texts

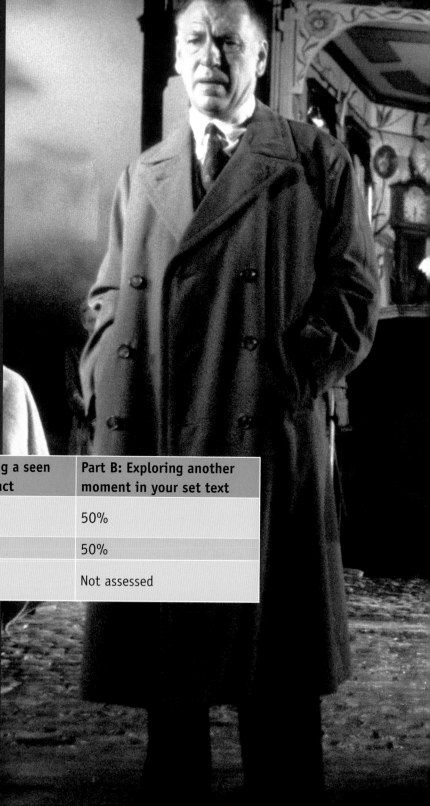

Component Overview

You will study one novel or play and prepare to answer one question (split into two parts) in Paper 1, Section A: Modern prose or drama.

- These two parts are worth 20 marks each, and together are worth a quarter of your total GCSE mark.

- Your first question, Part A, will ask you to compare an extract from your set text with an *unseen extract* from a different text of the same genre.

- Your second question, Part B, will ask you to explore a different moment from your set text where characters or themes relate to the extract presented in the Part A question.

- The mark scheme for this exam divides marks between the Assessment Objectives as follows:

Assessment Objective	Part A: Comparing a seen and unseen extract	Part B: Exploring another moment in your set text
AO1: Critical interpretation and textual support	40%	50%
AO2: Language analysis	20%	50%
AO3: Understanding of context	40%	Not assessed

Novels

Animal Farm, George Orwell's political fairytale

Never Let Me Go, Kazuo Ishiguro's science fiction horror tale

Anita and Me, Meera Syal's bildungsroman about a British Indian family

Plays

An Inspector Calls, JB Priestley's supernatural detective story

DNA, Dennis Kelly's bleak shocker

My Mother Said I Never Should, Charlotte Keatley's exploration of mother/daughter heartache

You need to study one novel *or* one play.

You should also read widely in the genre of the set text you are studying in preparation for the unseen comparison question in Part A of the exam.

Quotation Bank

You will not be able to take your text into the exam, so you are encouraged to build a bank of quotations as you read your set text. Find quotations that show different sides of a character, and how a theme develops.

Activity

1. Choose one character from your set text.

2. Find and write down quotations from the opening chapter or scene of the text that reveal something about the character you have chosen.

3. Now write down quotations from the final chapter or scene of the text that reveal something about the character.

4. Can you detect any ways in which the character has developed by the end?

Unit 1 How do you study modern prose and drama?

Learning objectives

- To identify aspects of the genres and key features of each
- To analyse how writers use form and structure to create effects and impact

Prose and drama have a lot in common, for example, character, setting and plot. What sets the two genres apart is how these aspects are presented.

Key features of drama texts

Plays are written to be performed before a live audience and present a story through lines of dialogue between characters. The text of a play is called a script.

Plays are divided into acts, which are then sub-divided into scenes. Lines in scripts are often numbered.

Stage directions tell directors how to stage the play. For instance, they can tell actors when to exit and enter, or how to deliver a line. There is an example from *An Inspector Calls* below:

> **MRS BIRLING** [triumphantly] Didn't I tell you?

They can tell directors how lighting should be used or where actors should stand on stage. At the start of an act or scene, stage directions might say how the stage should look. This is called the **'at-rise' description**.

Dramatic tension is the tension and suspense a playwright creates on stage. For example, Inspector Goole states firmly that he will deal with one line of enquiry at a time in J. B. Priestley's *An Inspector Calls*. We, the audience, have to wait for the outcome of the investigation, as well as the Birlings, thus the dramatic tension builds.

Dramatic irony exists when the audience knows something that the characters on stage do not. For example, *An Inspector Calls* is set in 1912, so when Mr Birling shrugs off talk of labour troubles, an audience in 1945 would know that the working classes would soon mobilize and strike, and working people's rights would be won. Priestley uses dramatic irony here to make fun of Mr Birling.

Tip

When writing about drama, talk about the effect on the audience; with prose, talk about the effect on the reader.

Key term

'At-rise' description how the stage looks when the curtain rises at the beginning of an act or a scene in a play

Activity 1

1. In small groups, find a section in the play you are studying where stage directions are used to tell the actors how to deliver the lines.

2. Change the stage directions and deliver the lines differently.

3. See if the class can guess what your new stage directions are.

4. As a group, discuss whether the story or characters have changed with the new directions.

Key features of prose

Prose is any kind of writing that is not a play or poetry. It is made up of sentences and paragraphs and can include novels, short stories, letters or essays. It can be fiction or non-fiction.

A novel is usually divided into chapters, sometimes with a prologue at the start.

A prologue can whet the reader's appetite by presenting the reader with an intriguing scene that makes them want to read on. Meera Syal's prologue in *Anita and Me* introduces us to Meena: we learn that apparently her mother put her in a newspaper-lined drawer when she was a baby and read all about Kennedy's assassination in the 'reversed newsprint' on Meena's 'damp backside'. We can see that this character has an edgy sense of humour and could *possibly* make up stories. We want to read more about her!

Novels not only use dialogue to tell a story, they use description, **imagery**, **symbolism**, **metaphor**, **simile**, **personification**, perspective and structure. So a novelist has a huge number of choices to make.

Activity 2

1. Re-read the opening paragraphs of your set text. What can you tell about the story's themes and characters based on this introduction?

2. Now rewrite the opening from the point of view of a different character.

3. Does the new perspective suggest anything different in terms of characters, themes or atmosphere?

Key terms

Imagery the use of descriptive or figurative language to help a reader visualize an idea

Symbol an object or sign which represents something else. This can be especially true of something physical representing something abstract. For instance, the symbol of justice is a pair of weighing scales

Metaphor when a writer describes something as if it *is* something else

Simile when a writer describes something as if it is *like* something else

Personification when a writer gives an inhuman thing human qualities, for example, 'The tree waved its arms in the wind'

Why are form and structure important?

In an interview, playwrights Richard Bean and Gill Adams give advice to aspiring playwrights:

Source text A

An interview with Richard Bean and Gill Adams for Hull Truck Theatre

Interviewer: What do you feel is the most important aspect of writing when approaching a new play?

Richard Bean: "Structure; a structure that will allow for an ending. Anyone can write the first act of a play, a good idea, a good location, a good situation; but the end is when you have a structure."

Interviewer: What one piece of advice would you give to any budding writer?

Gill Adams: "Believe that structure matters - Without it even a great story won't work. Get the structure right and it will make your story jump off the page."

As part of your English Literature GCSE you will analyse and evaluate how writers use form and structure to make the reader or the audience feel different emotions. Writers use structure to create effects. The same applies for form. You will need to think about why the writers have chosen one form over another and how they use the form to create an impact on the reader or the audience.

What is form?

Form is the type of writing chosen by the writer, for example, a play, a novel, a poem. Within these types of writing there are *more* forms. A novel could be written in the form of letters or as a diary. Whether the narrative voice is first, second or third person; what tense the story is told in; genre and its conventions; the mood or tone – these are all aspects of form.

Plays also have different forms. A play can be a tragedy where a protagonist such as Macbeth comes to a sticky end thanks to a tragic flaw in their character, or a comedy where the audience can laugh along with the characters.

Within plays there are other dramatic conventions: stage directions; soliloquy or monologue – when an actor speaks alone on stage; or asides when an actor makes a remark to the audience. These are all examples of dramatic form.

At the end of *An Inspector Calls*, J. B. Priestley shows the tension within the Birling family through stage directions that tell the actors how to deliver the dialogue. Sheila must speak *bitterly*, Mr Birling responds *angrily* to Eric, Mrs Birling speaks *warningly* to her husband. This is an example of how Priestley uses form to tell his story in such a way that it makes an impact. In *Animal Farm*, Orwell cannot use stage directions to tell his story because he is writing a novella. In order to create drama, Orwell uses the tools that are available to him in this form.

Orwell may not be able to use stage directions, but he can show the tension between characters through descriptive writing and a flurry of adjectives:

> [Squealer] cast a very ugly look at Boxer with his little twinkling eyes.

Notice how a similar relationship between characters can be expressed in drama or in prose, but the form determines *how* it is expressed.

What is structure?

This is the order in which the author chooses to tell the story. *An Inspector Calls* begins with an engagement party. *Animal Farm* ends with the pigs turning into human beings. When writing about structure, you should try to explain why the author orders the story this way.

Why does J. B. Priestley *choose* to begin *An Inspector Calls* in the Birlings' comfortable household, in the midst of an engagement party that will ally two powerful families? Why does Priestley choose to give the opening line to Arthur Birling as he takes the expensive port from his servant Edna, and passes it, boastfully, to his future son-in-law Gerald?

Possible answers might be to show the audience what is at stake for the Birlings should the Inspector's allegations become public knowledge; to show society's inequalities; to introduce the Birling family and what they represent. Can you think of any more reasons?

Tip
Structure can also relate to the structure of a sentence or a paragraph, a chapter or an act, as well as the novel or play as a whole.

Activity 3

What happens if you start your text at a different point in the story?

- *Never Let Me Go* at the point when Ruth undergoes her final donation
- *Animal Farm* with Snowball being chased from the farm
- *An Inspector Calls* with the Birling family in a state of shock, the Inspector having just left; the story could be told in flashback.

What does this change add, and what is lost?

Stretch

Can you reorder more of the story? Remember, your main aim is to engage the reader. How will the reordered set text do this? What did the author gain by using this structure?

17

How can I write about form and structure in the exam?

Read the extract below from *Punk Rock* by Simon Stephens. How does Simon Stephens use form and structure to create dramatic effects in the extract?

Source text B

Punk Rock by Simon Stephens

Sixth former William has committed an act of violence against his classmate, Nicholas. Here, he meets psychologist Dr Richard Harvey.

William I bet there are a million things you want to ask me, are there? Actually there are one thousand eight hundred things, eh? But I bet you want to know more than whether or not I feel confident in estate agents, don't you? Does it freak you out a bit being in here with me?

Dr Harvey No.

William Have you got a panic button?

Dr Harvey Yes I do.

William Is it underneath your desk? Have you got any children? Have you, Richard?

Dr Harvey I've a daughter.

William How old is she?

Dr Harvey She's seventeen.

William My age.

Does it make you sick what I did?

Does it make you sick what I did?

Dr Harvey No.

William You're lying. I can tell by the way you look to the left. When people look to the right they're thinking. When they look to the left they're lying.

Can I have a glass of water, please?

Dr Harvey Certainly.

He stands to leave.

William I'll just wait here.

Dr Harvey enjoys the joke.

He exits.

Some time.

Nicholas enters.

He sits opposite William.

> *William almost laughs. He stares at him.*
>
> **William** Nicholas? Nicky?
>
> *He goes to touch his face.*
>
> Are you OK? Are you dead?
>
> Does it hurt?
>
> *Did I hurt you?*
>
> I'm –
>
> **William** *starts to cry a little bit. He stops himself and rubs his eyes dry furiously.*

Tip

Make sure structure is covered by comparing one incident to another incident within the extract. Use phrases like 'at the beginning of the play/novel', 'at the end of the play/novel'.

How does Simon Stephens use form and structure to create dramatic effects in the extract? Imagine you are in a theatre watching this play. Can you find lines at the beginning, middle and end of the extract that would grip you?

Here's how you could structure an answer:

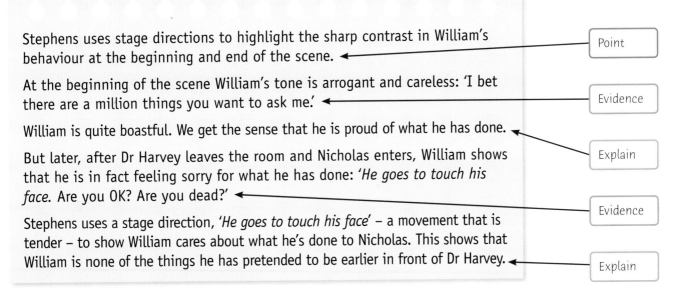

Stephens uses stage directions to highlight the sharp contrast in William's behaviour at the beginning and end of the scene. ← **Point**

At the beginning of the scene William's tone is arrogant and careless: 'I bet there are a million things you want to ask me.' ← **Evidence**

William is quite boastful. We get the sense that he is proud of what he has done. ← **Explain**

But later, after Dr Harvey leaves the room and Nicholas enters, William shows that he is in fact feeling sorry for what he has done: '*He goes to touch his face.* Are you OK? Are you dead?' ← **Evidence**

Stephens uses a stage direction, '*He goes to touch his face*' – a movement that is tender – to show William cares about what he's done to Nicholas. This shows that William is none of the things he has pretended to be earlier in front of Dr Harvey. ← **Explain**

Finally, *relate* it to the question. The sharp contrast between William's behaviour at the beginning and the end of the scene shocks the audience.

Activity 4

Find a scene in your set text where form and structure are used to create impact, and write a short paragraph explaining how the writer has achieved this effect. Remember to:

- make a **point**
- give **evidence** from the text
- **explain** how the evidence supports the point
- link back to the question by saying what **effect** the writer has achieved.

Key term

Genre the form of a literary text, such as a tragedy or comedy

Choice of genre

The form also reflects the **genre** of a text. The genre an author chooses to write in will affect the way the text is written and structured, whether to tell the story in the form of prose or as a poem or play. Depending on which they choose, the writer will have to use very different tools.

Source text C

About a Boy by Nick Hornby

Marcus has recently moved from Cambridge to London with his mother. He has just started a new school.

It wasn't all his mum's fault. Sometimes he was weird just because of who he was, rather than what she did. Like the singing... When was he going to learn about the singing? He always had a tune in his head, but every now and again, when he was nervous, the tune just sort of slipped out. For some reason he couldn't spot the difference between inside and outside, because there didn't seem to be a difference. It was like when you went swimming in a heated pool on a warm day, and you could get out of the water without noticing that you were getting out, because the temperatures were the same; that seemed to be what happened with the singing. Anyway, a song had slipped out yesterday during English, while the teacher was reading; if you wanted to make people laugh at you, really, really laugh, then the best way, he had discovered, better even than to have a bad haircut, was to sing out loud when everybody else in the room was quiet and bored.

Activity 5

Read the extract from Nick Hornby's novel *About a Boy* then follow the steps below to transform it into a play extract. Use as many dramatic conventions as you can: stage directions, dialogue, monologue, asides.

1. Read the whole extract. Note the main points that the writer is making. For example, Marcus is an outsider at his new school; Marcus is musical, etc.

2. Write a short play scene that delivers the same main points about Marcus.

    Think about: which parts of the extract will be most interesting to watch on stage; which characters need to speak on stage.

Stretch

Now choose a scene from your own set text and transform it from play to prose, or from prose to play. Once you have done so, write a short paragraph explaining how you have used form and structure to create impact.

Below is one example of how the novel extract could be transformed into a play.

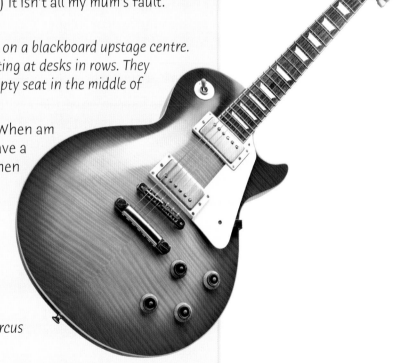

Marcus (*facing the audience, downstage right*) It isn't all my mum's fault. Sometimes I'm weird because of who I am.

Marcus glances behind him. A teacher is writing on a blackboard upstage centre. Centre stage are students in school uniform, sitting at desks in rows. They have their backs to the audience. There is an empty seat in the middle of the row nearest the audience.

Marcus (*as he walks towards the empty seat*) When am I going to learn about the singing? I always have a tune in my head. But every now and again, when I'm nervous, the tune just sort of slips out.

Marcus sits down with his back to the audience. The class is quiet. Some students have their heads on the desks, sleeping.

Beat.

Marcus sings out loud.

All the students turn in their seats and face Marcus (and the audience) and roar with laughter…

Unit 2 Understanding context

Learning objectives

- To use social, historical and literary context to help you understand the text

- To support your personal response to the text using your understanding of context

What is context?

Context is the background to the action. But it is more than that: context actually influences the action too, *shaping* events and characters.

Context affects you in your daily life too. Picture yourself first in class, and then at home. When you are in class, you are expected to wear a school uniform, not to speak when the teacher is speaking, to put your hand up when you want to answer a question. How does your behaviour change once you get home? This is an example of how context influences you. Can you think of other examples?

There are different kinds of context to look out for in your set text and the unseen extracts.

Social context	Examples
The way people behave or are treated in certain situations. Used to engage the reader, these are often situations we understand and are interested in.	• Meena's relationships with her parents in *Anita and Me* • The position of women in Britain in *An Inspector Calls* • The friendship between Tommy, Ruth and Kathy in *Never Let Me Go*
Cultural context	**Examples**
Traditions within cultures that feature in a text, or references to works of art, literature or monuments readers might recognize and be moved by.	• Meena's visit to the gurdwara in *Anita and Me* • Inspector Goole's use of biblical language when he refers to 'fire and blood' at the end of *An Inspector Calls*
Historical context	**Example**
What was happening at the time the text was written. Historical context can influence the writer's beliefs, the characters' behaviour and even the reader's response to a text.	• *An Inspector Calls* was written in 1945, just after the end of the Second World War, when many people would have felt strongly that humans needed to start caring more for each other.
Literary context	**Examples**
Novels and plays fall into different categories, called genres. If a text belongs to a specific genre, the reader expects it to contain certain features.	• *Anita and Me* is a coming-of-age story, and we expect Meena to grow and change throughout the story. • *An Inspector Calls* is a morality play and so delivers a moral lesson. • *An Inspector Calls* is also a detective story so it has lots of unexpected twists.

Activity 1

1. Re-read the definition of 'social context' on page 22.

2. Write down two examples of social context that relate to your set text, for example, the way in which a character is expected to behave towards his or her parents.

Activity 2

What genre do your set texts belong to? What do you expect to happen in texts that belong to these genres? For instance:

- *Anita and Me* is a *Bildungsroman*, a coming-of-age story with gothic elements
- *Never Let Me Go* is science fiction with a touch of gothic
- *An Inspector Calls* is a detective story and a moral tale with a few gothic elements
- *DNA* is a thriller, a moral tale and a comedy.

Context and character

Context is just another technique writers use to create effects. Let's go back to the example at the beginning of this unit. When you are at school, you are expected to behave in a certain way. But, does *everyone* follow *all* the school rules *all* of the time? A student might talk over the teacher or leave the classroom without permission. We can tell a lot about a person by the way they act in a particular context. Writers know this, and use context to illuminate their characters' personalities.

For example, Kazuo Ishiguro has Ruth in *Never Let Me Go* react in a particular way to a social context in order to *show* that she wants to fit in with her peers. When Kathy, Ruth and Tommy move from Hailsham to the Cottages, Ruth copies the veterans' mannerisms.

Source text A

Never Let Me Go by Kazuo Ishiguro

At the Cottages, though, when a couple were saying goodbye to each other, there'd be hardly any words, never mind embraces or kisses. Instead, you slapped your partner's arm near the elbow, lightly with the back of your knuckles, the way you might do to attract someone's attention. Usually the girl did it to the boy, just as they were moving apart. This custom had faded out by the winter, but when we arrived, it was what was going on and Ruth was soon doing it to Tommy.

Ishiguro does this to show how Ruth is not tied to Hailsham, like Kathy is. She wants to move on and fit in at the Cottages.

Activity 3

Think of an example of social context relating to your set text and answer the following questions.

1. Do the characters behave in a stereotypical or unusual way in this situation?

2. What is the writer telling us about their characters by having them act this way?

You might wish to use these examples:

Never Let Me Go: bullying at school; Tommy

An Inspector Calls: employer–employee relationship; Arthur Birling

Anita and Me: longing to fit in with the 'in-crowd'; Meena

Animal Farm: power relationships; Squealer

My Mother Said I Never Should: mother–daughter relationship; Jackie and Rosie

DNA: hierarchies among school pupils; Phil

Context and theme

Writers use context to develop themes and ideas. For example, Sheila Birling in *An Inspector Calls* defies her parents, saying it is unimportant whether Inspector Goole was a real Inspector or not; the fact is that the Birling family, between them, are responsible for Eva Smith's death. The social context here is *family relationships*. Priestley is playing with a social context we recognize to build the characters of Sheila and her parents. Sheila acts like an adult while her parents seem childish.

Priestley is *also* using social context to drive home his message about social responsibility. Caring about others is the *mature, adult* way to act, and behaving as if there is no such thing as community is *childish*.

Activity 4

In Activity 3, you thought about how context develops character. Now look at how it is also used to develop themes.

There are some examples in the table below to get you started.

Text	Context	Theme	How context helps the theme develop
Never Let Me Go	Bullying at school	The importance of art	Tommy is bullied at school because art is seen as important at Hailsham.
An Inspector Calls	Employer–employee relationship	Our responsibility for each other	Arthur Birling fires Eva and this is the start of her downfall (and his family's).
Anita and Me	Longing to fit in with the 'in-crowd'	Meena feels that she doesn't fit into British or Indian culture	Anita's racism makes Meena see she doesn't belong in the 'in-crowd'.
Animal Farm	Power relationships	The animals are responsible for their fate	The animals believe Squealer's lies and put their doubts aside.
My Mother Said I Never Should	Mother–daughter relationship	Family obligation versus career	Rosie resents Jackie for giving her up; but Jackie has a successful career.
DNA	Hierarchies among school pupils	Fear	Phil is feared by the other gang members.

How does the writer use context to develop other themes in your set text?

Context and the audience's emotions

Historical context determines what the writer writes; it also determines how the reader reads or interprets the text. Make sure you emphasize the *second* aspect. Writers second guess how a contemporary audience will react to their historical context. Always consider when the text is set, and when it was first published or performed.

Priestley uses historical context to build his characters, and make his audience feel a certain way about them. For instance, *An Inspector Calls* is set in 1912, when women had few rights in British society. His audience realizes how brave (even pioneering) Eva Smith was when she demanded a wage increase. Historical context increases our admiration for Eva Smith and our resentment of the Birlings for destroying her.

Tip

Remember, a context (probably social) will be highlighted in the comparison question. For example, for 'how is conflict between parents and their children presented in the two extracts?', underline the social context mentioned and relate what you say about language, structure and form to it in your answer.

Activity 5

1. Research the historical context of your set text: when it was written or when it is set.

2. What effect does the historical context have on the action of the book, and on the readers or the audience, then and now? For example:

   - Dennis Kelly chose not to tie *DNA* to a specific time or place. Why has Dennis Kelly chosen to do this?

   - *Anita and Me* is set in the 1970s. Have attitudes to race changed? Do we find the racism shocking? If the book had been published in the 1970s, would readers' reactions have been different to ours today?

How to write about context

The golden rule is to keep the text at the *centre* of what you say when discussing context. Focus on *how* the writer is using context to create effects. For instance, readers recognize that *Animal Farm* is an allegory and so a layer of power is added to Orwell's writing. Boxer is a symbol of the loyal working classes, who believed in the revolution. When he is sent to his death, we see the betrayal of the working classes. It is much more poignant, moving and powerful than if this were simply a fairytale about talking animals.

Activity 6

Read the opening of J. G. Ballard's short story 'Passport to Eternity' on page 27 and then answer the questions below.

1. Can you match these social contexts to the correct lines: class divides between rich and poor; married couples; competition with other couples?

2. Think of two other social contexts and find lines that relate to them.

3. What do these contexts help to reveal about the character of Margot? Can you complete the table?

Context	How Margot behaves	What this tells us about her
Class divides between rich and poor	Glum silence compared to revelry outside	She does not appreciate life's simple pleasures
Married couples	She is silent	
Competition with other couples		

Stretch

Explore what social contexts reveal about Clifford's character.

'Passport to Eternity' by J. G. Ballard

It was half past love on New Day in Zenith and the clocks were striking heaven. All over the city the sounds of revelry echoed upwards into the dazzling Martian night, but high on Sunset Ridge, among the mansions of the rich, Margot and Clifford Gorrell faced each other in glum silence.

Frowning, Margot flipped impatiently through the vacation brochure on her lap, then tossed it away with an elaborate gesture of despair.

'But Clifford, why do we have to go to the same place every summer? I'd like to do something interesting for a change. This year the Lovatts are going to the Venus Fashion Festival, and Bobo and Peter Anders have just booked into the fire beaches at Saturn. They'll all have a wonderful time, while we're quietly taking the last boat to nowhere.'

Activity 7

Can you answer the following question?

How are the rich presented in the extract from 'Passport to Eternity'?

A model answer has been started below.

The rich are presented as removed from the masses. ← Point

They are 'high' above the parties being held to celebrate 'New Day'. ← Evidence

Margot is literally above all the partying of the poorer members of society. ← Explain

But she is unhappy because of her snobbery. She faces her husband in 'glum silence'. This contrasts with the 'sounds of revelry' and the positive associations of the words 'love' and 'heaven'. ← Develop

Can you try to write a similar answer on your set text, using your notes from Activities 3 and 4?

Unit 3 Exploring meaning

Learning objectives

- To know how to look for meaning beneath the surface of a text
- To understand how language and setting shape meaning
- To identify meaning by linking different parts of a text

Key terms

Infer to conclude a meaning which is not explicitly stated

Didactic when a play, novel or speech teaches a specific lesson

How to look for meaning

When we look at the meaning of a text we have to read *between* the lines and work out what the writer is implying. When you work out the hidden meaning, you are demonstrating inference skills. To **infer** means to understand something without it being said.

Working out the author's purpose

To work out the meaning of different parts of your set text, first ask yourself, 'What is the author's purpose for writing the scene?'

Sometimes, the purpose of a scene is to develop a theme or build a character. In *Anita and Me*, when Meena sings 'We Wear Short Shorts' in front of her extended family, we see or infer how confident and outgoing Meena is, how she is caught between two cultures, and how she can shock her family.

In some cases, the text might be **didactic**. This means it aims to teach its audience or the reader a specific lesson. *An Inspector Calls* is the most obviously didactic text. J. B. Priestley implies that we are all part of a community and that our actions impact on others.

Keep the author's purpose at the forefront of your mind when looking for meaning in the text.

Setting

Writers choose settings for specific reasons. Always ask yourself, 'Why is the action happening here?'

In *An Inspector Calls*, Sheila mistreats Eva Smith in a clothes shop. Why does Priestley choose to set the scene *there*? You might say it is because, in 1912, women had few rights. If they wanted to get on in the world, they needed to marry well. Perhaps Sheila spent all her time in clothes shops, trying to make herself look appealing, because she couldn't do a lot else.

Activity 1

Identify other settings in your set text and suggest why the author chose to set the action there. Remember to ask yourself the following questions.

1. Does the setting tell me something about a character?
2. Does the setting link to a theme?
3. Is the author trying to teach me a lesson by using this setting?

   Here are some examples to get you started:

 Never Let Me Go: Ruth discovers that the woman they track down is not her 'possible', in an **art gallery**.

 An Inspector Calls takes place in Arthur Birling's home, in the **dining room**.

 Anita and Me: Meena witnesses Sam Lowbridge's racism at the **village fete**.

Symbolism

Events, characters, settings and any other aspect of a text can be symbolic of a bigger idea.

For example, J. B. Priestley uses stage directions symbolically. He does this to *show* the audience the dynamic between Eric and the rest of his family. The at-rise description reads:

> *'...the four* BIRLINGS *and* GERALD *are seated at the table, with* ARTHUR BIRLING *at one end, his wife at the other,* ERIC *downstage, and* SHEILA *and* GERALD *seated upstage...'*

Because Priestley has chosen to seat Eric away from the rest of his family, we can infer that Eric is a misfit in his family.

Activity 2

Can you find more examples of symbolism in your set text?

Here are some examples to get you started:

My Mother Said I Never Should: Rosie playing solitaire

DNA: Leah's 'bonobo' monologue

3

An Inspector Calls: the character of Eva Smith

Animal Farm: the pigs transforming into humans

Anita and Me: when Meena falls from Sherrie's horse and breaks her leg

6

Never Let Me Go: the marooned boat

What do these symbols represent? Remember to ask yourself the following questions.

1. Does this symbolize something about the nature of a character?
2. Does this symbolize a recurring theme?

Key terms

Imperative expressing a command

Tone how the attitude of a character or writer is portrayed in the language, for example, Inspector Goole's tone is authoritative; Meera Syal's tone in *Anita and Me* is comic

Exploring character and theme

The building blocks of character

Writers can build characters in a variety of ways. For example, let's look at how J. B. Priestley presents the characters of *An Inspector Calls*.

- Language: the cluster of **imperatives** the Inspector uses at the end of *An Inspector Calls* when he admonishes the Birlings – 'Remember that. Never forget it… Remember what you did' – gives the Inspector an authoritative **tone**.

- Stage directions: when Gerald and Eric try to glimpse the photograph he is showing to Mr Birling – '*the* INSPECTOR *interposes himself between them and the photograph*'. This shows the Inspector is assertive.

- Setting: the Birling's house is 'substantial and heavily comfortable, but not cosy and homelike'. This reflects the character of Mr Birling, who is not paternal or loving towards Eric, and is equally dismissive when Sheila crosses him.

Complex characters

The most interesting characters behave in contradictory ways. If you are exploring a character in an essay, try to show all sides of the character. One of the ways you can develop the points you make about a character is to mention the *other* ways they behave. For example:

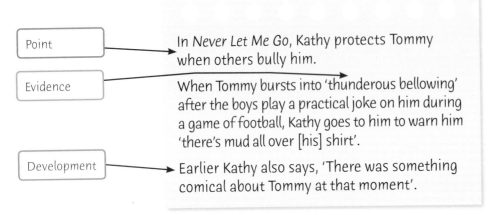

Point

In *Never Let Me Go*, Kathy protects Tommy when others bully him.

Evidence

When Tommy bursts into 'thunderous bellowing' after the boys play a practical joke on him during a game of football, Kathy goes to him to warn him 'there's mud all over [his] shirt'.

Development

Earlier Kathy also says, 'There was something comical about Tommy at that moment'.

Activity 3

Choose a character from your set text and write a list of their characteristics. Find a point in the text where the writer shows us a particular characteristic. What technique has the author used to show it?

The building blocks of theme

Themes are ideas that the writer develops through the course of the play or novel.

As with characters, writers can build or highlight themes in various ways. Meera Syal uses symbolism to highlight an important theme in *Anita and Me*. Meena's primary school is being demolished. It is up to you to make the connection between the demolition of Meena's primary school, leaving her childhood behind, and her growing up to learn about racism, her heritage, the value of family, and the shallowness of some friendships.

Writers can use their characters' words to build a theme too. For instance, the major theme in *An Inspector Calls* is the importance of working together as a community. Mr Birling is the first to take up this idea. Speaking as 'a hard-headed, practical man of business' he is against 'community and all that nonsense'. However, the Inspector says 'We don't live alone. We are members of one body. We are responsible for each other.'

Activity 4

Think of the text as a place where a writer conducts a debate. Different characters can offer different viewpoints on a topic: an example of this in *Never Let Me Go* is explored in the spider diagram below.

1. Debate a theme from your set text.
2. Debate another theme or the same theme while role-playing the different characters, putting forward their viewpoints.

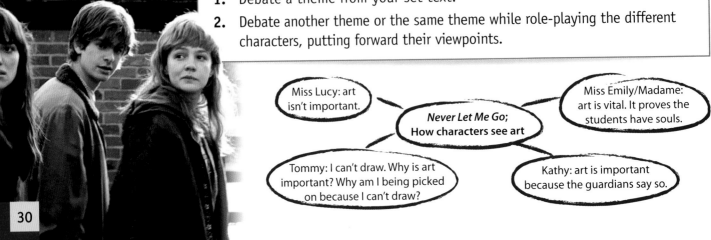

Miss Lucy: art isn't important.

Miss Emily/Madame: art is vital. It proves the students have souls.

Never Let Me Go; How characters see art

Tommy: I can't draw. Why is art important? Why am I being picked on because I can't draw?

Kathy: art is important because the guardians say so.

How to make links and connections with the rest of the text

Character development and motivation

Characters often grow during stories. In order to chart a character's development you need to make links *within* the text. To help you do this, note key quotations about characters as you read the text: what they say, what other characters say about them, how they behave.

For instance, Leah in *DNA* develops. At first she is desperate for Phil's attention. '*She strangles herself, her face turning red*', but Phil ignores her. Later, she threatens to run away, but '*drops her suitcase and sits with* PHIL' instead. Finally she '*Gets up, stares at* PHIL. *Storms off.*' She is no longer desperate for his attention.

After you have said how a character develops, then you need to say *why* they develop. You need to make more links within the text as you search for explanations as to why characters behave the way they do.

For example, why does Leah leave in Act 3? The answer is in Act 1. She believes she is connected to Phil: 'if you're thinking it might just have been him [Phil], on his own, without me, well that's not, we are completely, I am responsible as much as he…' She leaves after Phil orders Adam's execution because, if she stays, she will be responsible for Adam's death too.

Activity 5

Choose a line from your set text where a character behaves in a certain way. Explore those characteristics by finding another quotation that shows that behaviour.

For example: Sheila's line from Act 3 of *An Inspector Calls* shows the Inspector's impact on her: 'I remember what he said, how he looked, and what he made me feel. Fire and blood and anguish.'

An explanation for this behaviour could be when the Inspector says to Mrs Birling in Act 2: 'We often do [make a great impression] on the young ones. They're more impressionable.'

Stretch

Identify a character in your set text who you think has developed by the end.

1. Make a list of the key ways in which they develop.

2. Then say why they have developed.

3. Ask yourself, does the change help to highlight a key theme or message?

Thematic development

You can use the same technique to chart a theme's development as you do a character's. Write the title of a theme and then note key quotations connected to this theme as you read your text. Soon, you should be able to see how the theme develops.

Unit 4 Analysing language

Learning objectives

- To explain and show how language choices shape meaning
- To analyse how the writer uses language to create effects and impact
- To use technical terms when describing language features

The multiple effects of language

Writers are magicians, their stories portals into other worlds. Different techniques are used to create the magical effects we feel when reading or watching a play. We've seen how some magic is created through the way a writer uses form, structure, setting and different kinds of context. *Language* is another tool writers use to create effects.

Writers can use language to create a certain tone. For example, Meera Syal creates a comic tone in the prologue to *Anita and Me*.

> ### Source text A
>
> My parents... standing in the doorway of a 747, blinking back tears of gratitude and heartbreak as the fog cleared to reveal the sign they had been waiting for, dreaming of, the sign planted in tarmac and emblazoned in triumphant hues of red, blue and white that said simply, WELCOME TO BRITAIN.

The author uses **bathos** here. The sign her parents have been 'dreaming of' sounds glorious – 'emblazoned in triumphant hues' – but the image is not to be taken seriously as the sign is 'planted in tarmac'.

'Emblazoned' and 'triumphant' suggest military victories and point to the idea of colonialism.

Language can create **atmosphere** too. For example, through his verb choices, Orwell creates a fearful atmosphere when Napoleon orders the executions in *Animal Farm*: 'cowered', 'squealing', 'trembling'.

Language choices can reveal how a character is feeling. In *Anita and Me*, Meena says she 'scuttled' after her father as he whisked her to Mr Ormerod's sweet shop to uncover the truth about whether she paid for some sweets with money stolen from her mother's purse. Animals scuttle. *Small* animals. The word 'scuttle' tells us Meena feels ashamed.

Language can build a character too. In the previous unit, we mentioned how Inspector Goole speaks in imperatives, thus establishing him as an authoritative figure.

Key terms

Bathos when an outcome is so unexpected or disappointing that it becomes comical

Atmosphere a feeling or tone created by imagery and language

Analysis of language features and their effects

Grammatical features

This refers to how a writer structures their sentences. Try to say *why* they have chosen these structures. Why do they put a **subordinate clause** before a **main clause**? Why do they use **compound** or **complex sentences**?

For instance, in *An Inspector Calls* Inspector Goole uses a compound sentence and a simple sentence when he tries to explain that Eva Smith being fired could have led to her death:

> "Because what happened to her then may have determined what happened to her afterwards, and what happened to her afterwards may have driven her to suicide. A chain of events."

You could analyse this grammatical feature like this: The compound sentence, including the connective 'and', mirrors the 'chain of events'.

Literary features

Literary features include metaphor, simile, alliteration, **figurative language**, **satire**, **irony** and **anaphora**. Notice that language features, whether grammatical or literary, can have different effects at different points in the text. Pay close attention to the context. Ask yourself what is the effect at *this point* in the text.

For instance, Meera Syal uses anaphora to achieve different effects in *Anita and Me*:

> '… all that potential, all that hope, all gone because I made friends once with Anita Rutter'.

Here the technique emphasizes that Meena lost a lot because of something insignificant. It creates a hopeless tone.

A little earlier, anaphora shows how fed up Meena is and creates an angry tone:

> 'I hated Tracey for coming to my door, hated Anita for speaking to me all those years ago…, hated Sam for not being cruel to me… and mainly hated myself…'.

And before that, anaphora creates an almost comic tone. The news of Tracey's near-death experience is:

> 'broadcast on every corner, over every wall and fence, every intimate detail shared…'.

Subordinate clause the part of the sentence which is dependent on the main clause for its meaning and cannot stand on its own

Main clause a clause that can stand alone as a sentence

Compound sentence linking two simple sentences by a connective, for example: *and, but, however*

Complex sentence a sentence containing a subordinate clause or clauses

Figurative language language used to describe by comparing it to something else, using words not to be taken literally, such as in metaphors and similes

Satire when an important person or organization is made fun of

Irony when the surface meaning is opposite to the intended meaning, like sarcasm, but when nobody is insulted

Anaphora the repetition of a word or phrase at the beginning of successive clauses

Verisimilitude
a realistic, lifelike, or natural quality to language, such as when sensory language connected with sight, sound or smell creates verisimilitude

How to write about language and its effects

You also need to show that you understand *why* the writer is keen to create particular effects. It might be to establish a certain kind of atmosphere. It could be to build a character. Or highlight a theme. It could be to add **verisimilitude** to a setting.

Remember to structure your answers in the following way.

1. *Make a point*: say which language feature the writer is using and summarize why the writer uses it.

2. *Give evidence*: it can either be a full or embedded quotation.

3. *Explain* the evidence: say what the effect of the language feature is.

4. *Explain* why the writer wants to create this effect.

Sample analysis of sentence structure

Let's comment on the sentence structure in this extract from *Never Let Me Go*.

> 'It had become obvious to me by then, from the way the doctors, the co-ordinator, the nurses were behaving, that they didn't think she was going to make it.'

- Breaking up the main clause lessens its impact.

- This downplaying of things is characteristic of Kathy.

- Alternatively, you could say it gently builds tension in one of the most disturbing passages of the book, when Ruth dies.

How to write about this in the exam

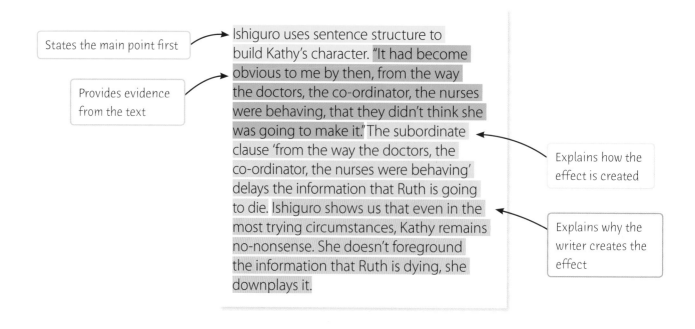

States the main point first

Provides evidence from the text

Ishiguro uses sentence structure to build Kathy's character. "It had become obvious to me by then, from the way the doctors, the co-ordinator, the nurses were behaving, that they didn't think she was going to make it." The subordinate clause 'from the way the doctors, the co-ordinator, the nurses were behaving' delays the information that Ruth is going to die. Ishiguro shows us that even in the most trying circumstances, Kathy remains no-nonsense. She doesn't foreground the information that Ruth is dying, she downplays it.

Explains how the effect is created

Explains why the writer creates the effect

Activity 1

Use the following quote, also from *Never Let Me Go*, to describe a different effect created by the same grammatical feature.

'Peering past her, I saw that the hallway, narrow as it was, divided further...'

- By putting the subordinate clause first, the layout of the house is revealed more gradually to us.

- Our perspective mirrors Kathy's: we're seeing the house as she does.

- This builds tension in the climax of the book, when Kathy and Tommy learn the truth about Hailsham.

- This build-up of tension is fitting for a scene that borrows from the **gothic** genre.

Turn the notes above into a short paragraph commenting on language. Remember to:

- state your main point first
- provide evidence
- explain *how* the effect is created
- explain *why* the effect is created.

Key term

Gothic a genre of fiction that is designed to unsettle; one of its features is old buildings with secret passageways, winding staircases and narrow hallways

Activity 2

Choose a passage from your set text that includes interesting language.

1. Identify the features of language that you think are significant. These could be literary or grammatical features.

2. For each feature, answer the following question:

Why has the author used this type of language at this point in the text?

Remember to structure your writing by making a point about language, giving evidence, explaining the effect, and explaining why the author wants to create this effect.

Unit 5 Making comparisons

Learning objectives

- To make contrasts between texts, comparing features and qualities

- To understand that comparing the set text to an unseen text can lead to a deeper understanding of the set text

- To learn to write effectively about links between texts

In the exam, you will be asked to compare a short extract from your set text with an unseen extract of the same genre (prose or drama). The question will ask you to consider how the *contexts* of the two extracts are presented. The question will probably mention a context, and give you a starting point for comparison. It could be a familiar social context, for example, family relationships or relationships at school. A question might read:

> *Anita and Me* by Meera Syal and *About a Boy* by Nick Hornby
>
> Compare how relationships at home and at school are presented in the two extracts.
>
> You should consider:
>
> - The situations and experiences faced by the characters
> - How the characters react to the situations and experiences
> - How the writers' use of language and techniques creates effects
>
> [20]

The question is asking you to focus on three areas in your answer.

The first bullet targets AO3 (context). 'Situations and experiences' is another way of saying *context*. It keeps you focused on the question.

The second bullet targets AO1 (themes and characters). 'How the characters react' is encouraging you to answer the question in more depth; it wants you to explore the context by considering how the characters in the text behave within it.

The third bullet targets AO2 (language, form and structure). The 'writers' use of language and techniques' to create effects is helping you to focus on the 'how relationships are presented' part of the question. Deal with it while you are addressing the first two bullets. In other words, explore how the situations and experiences (first bullet) and the characters' reactions (second bullet) are presented using language features and techniques.

Tip

In your exam question, the bullets are there to help you write a good answer.

Comparing two texts

Read the extract below from *Anita and Me* and compare it to the extract from *About a Boy* on page 20 (Unit 1).

(on page 20 (Unit 1))

Source text A

Anita and Me by Meera Syal

Meena performs a song she has heard on the television at a mehfil, *a gathering of friends and family at her parents' home.*

'Okay,' I said, took a deep breath and launched into a rendition of 'We Wear Short Shorts', complete with the gyrating dance routine I had seen Pan's People do to it on *Top Of the Pops*. I flicked my hair and kicked my legs as papa and Uncle Tendon gamely tried to match a key and rhythm to my show stopper, although their complex minor key riffs and passionate drum solos did not altogether complement the song. I finished by shouting 'Yeah man!', and doing the splits, accompanied by a loud ripping noise and after a moment's pause, a round of enthusiastic applause. Mama pulled me up and examined the large tear along the crotch of my trousers. 'Did you have to do that?' she hissed.

Papa laughed, 'Leave her! It was very groovy, Meena! That was what you call a good jam-in, hey Tendon saab?'

They slapped each other's backs and hooted uproariously.

The Aunties and Uncles just loved me; they crowded round patting me like a pet, over-enthusing about my talent and charisma whilst papa shot knowing winks to mama, who was slowly melting in the face of this public approval.

By pairing these two extracts, our understanding of the *Anita and Me* extract is enhanced. Meena sings freely, and Marcus doesn't. When comparing two extracts, we ask why. It's due to context: Marcus is at a new school, where he is not fitting in; Meena is at home, surrounded by a warm, loving family. Context determines Meena and Marcus's behaviour; likewise it determines the behaviour of the characters around them.

How to write a comparison

The following activity will give you a framework that you can use when you are comparing two texts. It is based on the extracts from *Anita and Me* and *About a Boy* but the approach can be applied to your own texts.

Activity 1

1. Read through each extract and make a list of the situations and experiences in each. This covers the first bullet point of the question. Here are some ideas to get you started. You might like to record your ideas in a table like the one below.

1ST POINT: Situations/ experiences	2ND POINT: Reactions	EVIDENCE: Language/ techniques	EXPLAIN: Effects
Meena sings at home			
Marcus sings at school			
Meena's singing is praised			

Use the ideas that you have noted down to compare and contrast the situations and experiences in the extracts, for example:

> Meena sings at home and Marcus sings at school.

2. To *improve* your point, tackle the second bullet point at the same time. For each point you made above, make a note of the characters' reactions to the situations. Add these to column 2 of your table.

Now write a point which takes into account the situation the character faces *and* their reaction to it, for example:

> Meena sings at home and is uninhibited as a result, whereas Marcus sings at school and is humiliated as a result.

3. Next, address the third bullet point: the language and techniques used by the writer. Add the evidence for your point in column 3 of your table. Try to embed the evidence in the sentence where you make your point using key words from the text rather than whole sentences.

States the main point first

Meena sings at home and is uninhibited as a result. She 'flicked' her hair and 'kicked' her legs. In contrast, Marcus sings at school and is humiliated as a result. His classmates 'laugh' at him; 'really, really laugh'.

Provides evidence from the text

4. Finally, explain the effect of the language or technique. In other words, explain the evidence you're using to support your point. Add this to column 4.

Provides evidence from the text

States the main point first

Meena sings at home and is uninhibited as a result. She 'flicked' her hair and 'kicked' her legs; two powerful verbs that emphasize her energy. Whereas Marcus sings at school and is humiliated as a result. His classmates 'laugh' at him; 'really, really laugh'. The repetition of laugh emphasizes just how humiliated Marcus was by the students' reaction.

Explains how the effect is created and how the evidence supports the point

Activity 2

Choose one of the following.

1. Continue the comparison activity started above:

> Compare how relationships at home and at school are presented in the two extracts from *Anita and Me* by Meera Syal and *About a Boy* by Nick Hornby.
>
> You should consider:
>
> - The situations and experiences faced by the characters
> - How the characters react to the situations and experiences
> - How the writers' use of language and techniques creates effects

2. Ask your teacher to provide you with a pair of texts to compare. One should be an extract from your set text. Make notes to help you answer the following exam-style question:

> How do the writers present similar social contexts in the two extracts?
>
> You should consider:
>
> - The situations and/or experiences faced by the characters
> - The characters' reactions
> - The language and techniques used by the writers

Unit 6 Getting ready for the exam

Learning objectives

- To respond personally and critically to a text and support writing with evidence
- To write about language, form and structure using technical terms
- To write about how texts relate to social, historical and literary contexts

Key term

Active reading
reading something to understand and evaluate it for its relevance to your needs, for example, underlining key phrases that relate to the exam question

The exam question

In the exam, you will be asked a two-part question.

- Part A will ask you to compare an extract from your set text with an extract from an unseen text.
- Part B will ask you to explore a different moment in your set text that relates to the two extracts you have compared in Part A.

You will be assessed on each exam question as follows:

Assessment Objective		Part A: comparing a seen and unseen extract	Part B: exploring another moment in your set text
A01:	**Critical interpretation** and textual support	40%	50%
A02:	**Language analysis**	20%	50%
A03:	Understanding of **context**	40%	Not assessed

Planning your response to Part A

You are advised to spend 45 minutes on Part A: 10 minutes **actively reading** the two extracts, 5 minutes planning, and 25 minutes writing your answer. Spend the final 5 minutes checking spelling and grammar.

Step 1: Read the question and circle the words relating to context. An example of this has been completed below:

---

1. *My Mother Said I Never Should* by Charlotte Keatley and *Grief* by Mike Leigh

    a. Compare how conflict between mothers and daughters is presented in the two extracts. You should consider:
       - The situations and experiences faced by the characters
       - How the characters react to their situations
       - How language and dramatic features create effects

       [20]

My Mother Said I Never Should by Charlotte Keatley

Rosie has discovered that her 'sister' Jackie is, in fact, her mother. In this scene, Jackie explains to Rosie why she gave her up and allowed her own mother, Margaret, to raise her.

Grief by Mike Leigh

Dorothy has returned home to find her daughter, Victoria, at home instead of at school. Victoria tells her mother she has come home because she has a headache.

If you do this, you will have a head start. You will already know the social context is relationships between mothers and daughters; and while Jackie is on the defensive, *explaining*, Victoria is more in control, *telling* her mother what's what.

Step 2: Read the set text extract first and highlight the parts that relate to the situations and experiences faced by the characters and number them. An example of this has been completed below:

Source text A

My Mother Said I Never Should by Charlotte Keatley

Rosie If you were really my Mum you wouldn't have been able to give me away! **(1)**

Jackie How dare you! (*Goes to hit* **Rosie** *but cannot*.) You're at the centre of everything I do! (*Slight pause*.) Mummy treated me as though I'd simply fallen over and cut my knee, – picked me up and said you'll be all right now, it won't show much. **(2)** She wanted to make it all better. (*Quiet*.)... She was the one who wanted it kept secret... I WANTED you, Rosie. **(3)** (*Angry*.) For the first time in my life I took care of myself – refused joints, did exercises, went to the clinic. (*Pause*.) 'It's a girl'. (*Smiles irresistibly*.) – After you'd gone I tried to lose that memory. (*Pause. Effort*.) Graham... your Father. (*Silence*.) He couldn't be there the day you were born, **(4)** he had to be in Liverpool. He was married. **(5)** (*Emphatic*.) He loved me, he loved you, you must believe that! [...] It was a very cold winter after you were born. There were power cuts. I couldn't keep the room warm; there were no lights in the tower blocks; [...] I phoned Mummy. (*Difficult*.) Asked her. (*Pause*.) I tried! I couldn't do it, Rosie. (*Pause*.) It doesn't matter how much you succeed afterwards, if you've failed once. (*Pause*.) [...] I could give you everything now. Rosie?...

Rosie (*pause*) I used to hate you, only I never knew why.

Activity 1

On your a copy of the extract, highlight more sections of source text A above relating to the situations and experiences the characters face. Next, circle parts relating to characters' reactions.

Some lines serve a double purpose. 'If you were really my Mum you wouldn't have been able to give me away!' tells us about the situation Rosie faces (she's been given up by her mother) and also tells us her reaction (she is bewildered by her mother's decision).

Grief by Mike Leigh

Dorothy Victoria, do you really have a headache?

Victoria (*standing up*) Yes, of course I have a headache, I'm not lying.

Dorothy I'm not suggesting that you are lying.

Victoria Yes, you are.

Dorothy No, I'm not.

Victoria You're calling me a liar.

Dorothy I'm merely trying to ascertain whether you do indeed have a headache ... or whether you've been playing truant.

Victoria How dare you accuse me of truanting? I have a terrible headache, and I came home early, and you weren't even here to look after me, and I've had to be on my own all afternoon.

Dorothy Yes, I'm sorry I wasn't here when you got back. I went up to the West End.

Victoria Why are you saying vile things to me? You're being horrible.

Dorothy No, I'm not, darling.

Victoria You're being completely unfair.

Dorothy Please, Victoria – please, I've never done anything other than look after you and love you.

Victoria Oh, stop it.

Dorothy Why are you so angry with me all the time? You used to be such a well-behaved little girl during the war. Your daddy would have been so proud of you.

Victoria Oh, don't bring Daddy into it! I never even knew him.

Dorothy I only ever try to do my best.

Victoria collects her things.

Victoria I hate you!

Key term

Nuance a finer, less obvious detail

Activity 2

Read the unseen extract opposite from the play *Grief*. Find lines to compare with ones you've highlighted in *My Mother Said I Never Should* on page 41.

1. Start with line (1) in *My Mother Said I Never Should*, which is highlighted yellow, for situations and experiences. Find a line that compares or contrasts with it in *Grief* and label that line (1) too.

   For instance, you could compare Rosie's 'If you were really my Mum you wouldn't have been able to give me away!' with Victoria's '...you weren't even here to look after me, and I've had to be on my own all afternoon'.

2. Continue and label as many parts of the unseen text as you can to show links with *My Mother Said I Never Should,* or your own set text.

Tips for both Part A and Part B

Using quotes and textual references

Keep quotes short, embedding only the key words in sentences.

For example: Rosie uses a conditional structure, saying 'if' Jackie had been her real mother she 'wouldn't have been able to give [her] away'. 'If' and 'wouldn't' are key as they show the conditional form.

Introductions

Start with a line that answers the question in a succinct, catchy way. Avoid generic lines like, 'The writers use interesting language techniques to talk about family relationships.' Be specific. If your introduction could be about *other* moments from *other* texts, try again! For example:

> Conflict is presented as rational by Keatley and irrational by Leigh ...

Then say briefly what the main contrasts and comparisons are between the two extracts.

Rosie is in control of the situation yet Jackie does all the talking; Victoria dominates but is in the wrong.

Activity 3

Can you add a few more lines to the above introduction that sum up other similarities and differences? Keep to five lines at most for an introduction.

Conclusions

Synthesize the points you have made in your essay in your conclusion. That means draw them together. Think of your introduction as a sum, and the conclusion as the answer to that sum. By the time you reach the conclusion, you should have explored the **nuances** in your opening line, for example, 'Conflict is presented as rational by Keatley and irrational by Leigh', so that your conclusion considers the grey areas in this black and white statement.

Activity 4

Plan your answer.

1

Plan your introduction and conclusion last (see below). Start with the main body of your answer.

2

Look at the situations and experiences you've highlighted. Decide on the best order to present them and write a list.

3

Next, look at character reactions. You can either:

- include these in the second half of your answer, after you have written about situations and experiences, or

- merge them with the first half by also discussing how characters relate to each situation or experience you mention.

4

Finally, jot down any notable language features employed by the writer, alongside each similarity or difference you have listed, in the lines you pair.

Tackling Part B

In the exam, you should spend 30 minutes on Part B: 5 minutes planning, 20 minutes writing, and 5 minutes at the end checking spelling and grammar.

The Part B question will ask you to explore another moment from your set text where similar ideas to those in Part A appear. For example:

> **b.** Explore another moment in the play that develops the theme of conflict between mothers and daughters.
>
> **[20]**

Being an explorer

When you're *exploring* a moment in your set text, imagine you are climbing a mountain nobody else has climbed.

For example: When Doris says 'Oh Mother, I'm so happy, SO HAPPY!' in the flashback at the end of *My Mother Said I Never Should,* it is the unhappiest moment in the play and to show this, you need to *explain* this quotation.

This evidence can be explained by saying: Doris is 'SO HAPPY' because she has received a marriage proposal. Keatley has made it clear throughout the play that marriage does not equal happiness. Doris admits to her daughter Margaret: 'Your Father … stopped "wanting me", many years ago.' Margaret's own husband, Ken, leaves her.

Use technical vocabulary for example: Structuring the play with this scene at the end loads Doris's words with irony and **pathos**.

Develop your points. This is another way of saying *explore*. You can develop an answer in all sorts of ways. 'However' is a good place to start. After you've made a point, offer an alternative interpretation.

For example: However, by the end of the play Doris is single and empowered. While her younger self is a pathetic, naive figure, she is also comic. Perhaps we can laugh with Doris at her younger self, 'SO HAPPY' to receive a marriage proposal.

Key term

Pathos a feeling of sympathy or compassion or pity

Tip

Use tentative language such as 'perhaps' or 'maybe' when offering alternative interpretations.

Sample student answers

Read the sample exam question and sample student answers below and on page 46 and 47. Complete Activity 5 on page 47.

---

1. *My Mother Said I Never Should* by Charlotte Keatley and *Grief* by Mike Leigh

   a. Compare how conflict between mothers and daughters is presented in the two extracts? You should consider:

   • The situations and experiences faced by the characters

   • How the characters react to their situations

   • How language and dramatic features create effects

   [20]

Student A

Rosie does not say very much in the extract, but we can tell she's angry. Jackie says more. She is explaining why she let her mother bring up Rosie. Jackie says: 'It was a very cold winter after you were born.' Victoria and her mother speak in the other extract. Victoria is angry with her mother because she thinks she is playing truant. Victoria overreacts and says that her mother is 'vile'.

This is a weak response. Context is mentioned, but the student does not say how it helps understanding of the extract. Both extracts are mentioned, and there is an attempt to link the two. Evidence is used to support a point, but on the whole the answer is paraphrasing the story. Language features and their effects are not dealt with.

Student B

Rosie's first line is full of different emotions. No wonder; it's a huge adjustment she is having to make, from a sisterly relationship with Jackie to mother and daughter. 'If you were really my Mum you wouldn't have been able to give me away!' expresses bewilderment through the use of a conditional. She even doubts Jackie is her mother: 'If you were <u>really</u> my Mum…' There are no stage directions for Rosie but the exclamation mark at the end of the sentence would allow an actor to deliver the line angrily. Victoria, on the other hand, is a less sympathetic character. Like Rosie, she knows a mother's role is to care for her daughter. She capitalizes on this, guilt-tripping her mother for not being at home when she comes back from school with 'a terrible headache'. Victoria uses polysyndeton to stress how many things her mother has done wrong: '<u>and</u> I came home early, <u>and</u> you weren't even here to look after me, <u>and</u> I've had to be on my own all afternoon'. Dorothy caves in, and says 'sorry'. Perhaps she believes it will be easier to back down because this will pacify her difficult daughter. Jackie, on the other hand, attempts to explain herself. This could reflect that Jackie and Rosie are on more equal ground. Actually, they are more like sisters.

This is a good answer. It shows an understanding of how the context (the expectations of what a parent–child relationship should be) informs the action. Technical terms are used when considering effects of language features. Quotes are embedded and support what is said. There is a perceptive comment when the candidate notes that Jackie and Rosie are more like sisters.

---

b. Choose one other moment where characters are in conflict with each other, and explore how the writer makes the moment dramatic.

[20]

Student A

Charlotte Keatley slowly builds tension between Margaret and Jackie in the scene when Margaret takes baby Rosie from Jackie. Before Margaret's entrance, the audience senses that Jackie feels her mother will judge her. Stage directions are used to show this. She '*Picks up ashtray*' as she tries to tidy Sandra and Hugh's mess from the other night. Dialogue is used too. She has 'Washed everything' she tells Rosie, '*Holding back tears*'. When Margaret enters, her third line is: 'You've been smoking.' It's a declarative and it sounds judgemental. Jackie ignores her, but the audience knows trouble is brewing. 'Don't wake her!' Jackie snaps. It's an imperative. Jackie wants to maintain some sort of control of the situation. 'Leave those!' she tells her mother when she tries to take Rosie's old clothes. And then her mother's frustrations erupt too. 'Why did you have to try!' The exclamation mark suggests she's exasperated. 'All by yourself?' Margaret still feels maternal towards Jackie. It makes her character more sympathetic as she is experiencing complex emotions too. This adds to the drama of the scene.

This is a good answer. It is a personal response supported by evidence, which is sharply focused on the question. The student explores how the writer makes the moment dramatic. How the writer uses language, structure and aspects of dramatic form such as stage directions and dialogue to create effects is considered, using relevant terminology.

Student B

The most dramatic moment in the play is when Jackie gives up her baby, Rosie, to her mother Margaret. Margaret tells Jackie not to tell Rosie the truth until she is 16. Jackie can carry on with her life now. Her mother says 'a year ago you had everything' and Jackie promises she will finish her degree. But Jackie doesn't want to give her baby up. She says it is just what her mother wants her to do. They are her mother's 'Expectations'.

This is a weaker answer. The candidate has included several points in one paragraph, rather than exploring each in more detail. One of the points is not made clearly as a result. There is no analysis of language, form and structure and how it creates dramatic effects, therefore the question has not been addressed.

Activity 5

- In pairs, rewrite the weaker answers above and on page 45, improving them based on the comments provided.
- Swap answers and mark each other's work.
- Has the answer you are marking responded to all the examiner's comments?

Progress check

Use this table to check how well you understand your modern text, and how confident you are that you can write an examination response which meets the assessment objectives.

	I still have some questions about this	I am sure I understand this	I am confident I can give clear explanations with examples
I understand the main differences between prose and drama.			
I understand how writers can use form to create effects.			
I understand how writers can use structure to create effects.			
I understand which kinds of context appear in my set text.			
I understand how context can be used to create effects.			
I can read between the lines in texts when I look for meaning.			
I understand how a writer can create characters.			
I understand how a writer can develop themes.			
I am familiar with many of language's different effects.			
I can write about language and its effects.			
I have a method that I use to compare texts.			
I feel confident that I can tackle Section A of the exam.			

2 19th-century prose

Component Overview

- You will study one 19th-century novel and answer one question in Paper 1, Section B: 19th-century prose.

- There is a choice of an extract-based question or a whole-text essay.

- The extract-based question requires you to look outside the extract and show whole text understanding.

- The essay question should be based on exploring two or three moments from the novel in close detail.

- There are 40 marks for the 19th-century prose question so it carries 50% of the marks for this paper.

- The mark scheme for this exam divides marks between the Assessment Objectives as follows:

Assessment Objective	% of marks
AO1: Critical interpretation and textual support	35%
AO2: Language analysis	35%
AO3: Understanding of context	20%
AO4: Vocabulary, Sentences, Spelling and Punctuation	10%

Set texts

You will be studying one of:

The Strange Case of Dr Jekyll and Mr Hyde
Robert Louis Stevenson

Great Expectations
Charles Dickens

The War of the Worlds
H.G.Wells

Jane Eyre
Charlotte Brontë

Pride and Prejudice
Jane Austen

Quotation Bank

As you study your 19th-century novel, you will be encouraged to assemble a quote bank on key characters and themes. You will be encouraged to link sections of the text and form a sound understanding of how your novel is structured.

Start to build your own quotation bank. Categorise your quotations into different themes and characters and display them around your classroom or create a revision booklet.

1. Choose one major theme or one major character from your set text.

2. Find and write down quotations from the opening chapter/s of the text that introduce the theme or character you have chosen.

3. Now find quotations from your text and trace the development of your theme or character.

4. Now write down quotations from the final chapter/s that indicate a resolution or the outcome for that theme or character.

5. Can you detect any ways in which the theme or character has developed throughout the novel?

Revision notes

Remember that you cannot take your text into the exam with you, as this is a 'closed book' examination. This means that you need to make useful notes throughout your study of the novel so that you can revise them effectively before the examination. These notes can be catagorised into:

- Knowledge of plot/events

- Short and precise quotations

- Themes – their significance and how they are linked in different parts of the text

- Language – how it is used to build up atmosphere, create attitudes and irony

- Characters – how they develop

- Settings – their significance.

You will create notes and diagrams on all the major characters and themes and how they relate to one another. You will also learn about the social, cultural and historical context of the novel you are studying so that you can understand how the world was different when it was written than it is today and how that impacts on the novel's meanings.

Unit 1 How do you study 19th-century prose?

Learning objectives

- To understand the genre of the 19th-century novel you are studying and key features of this genre
- To introduce the concept of form and **structure**
- To explore the role of the narrator

Key terms

Structure how a piece of writing is put together; how the choices of language, punctuation and form affect the message or meaning being conveyed

Genre the form of a literary text, such as a tragedy or comedy

Tip

Think about *how* the novel you are studying reflects or explores these changes and developments. You will be expected to show understanding of the social context in your exam responses.

Genres of 19th-century novels and how they relate to key features of the text

In the 19th century, lots of different styles of novels were popular. Some were realistic and challenged social conventions, whereas some told horror stories involving mysterious settings and frightening events. When you study a novel it is important to understand the **genre** it belongs to because each one has important features that you will learn to recognize as you get to know the text. It will also help you understand the meanings and themes of your text.

The 19th Century

The 19th Century in Britain was a time of great change and discovery and many of those changes and discoveries will be reflected or explored in the text you study. The developments you should be aware of are listed below.

- Political developments: the growth of the British Empire; industrial growth; the emergence of a more vocal working class; more calls for women's rights.

- Social developments: improvements in educational provision; limitation of child labour; changes to the social class structure; movement of the population from rural areas to cities and towns for work; a rapidly growing population.

- Scientific developments: discoveries and inventions such as the telephone, steam trains and motor cars; the growth of scientific knowledge and research.

- Cultural developments: the serialization of novels in publications; an interest in the supernatural; a fear of extraterrestrial life; the popularity of gothic horror stories.

Activity 1

Create a mind map showing how the 19th-century novel you are studying reflects the developments listed above. Link any developments with at least one character, setting or key point in your text.

What sorts of novels were published in the 19th century?

The 'novel of manners' *Pride and Prejudice,* written in 1813, is a good example of this genre. Jane Austen writes about the gentry of rural England. She uses gentle satire to mock social snobbery and silly behaviour. She also explores some serious issues, such as marriage and the effects of social hierarchies. Her novels are set in a narrow society, where people's behaviour is closely scrutinized. Her authorial voice is often evident in the novel as she passes judgement on the characters through the use of irony and mockery.

The 'novel of social criticism' *Great Expectations,* written in 1860, by Charles Dickens, explores many social issues, including crime and punishment, social hierarchies, the true notion of a gentleman, and whether money and wealth are more important than humanity and kindness to other people.

Both *Pride and Prejudice* and *Great Expectations* can also be classed as romantic novels, as both explore the idea of love. Either of these novels could also be called a *Bildungsroman* – a novel in which the central character 'comes of age' or grows up in front of the reader's eyes.

The War of the Worlds, written in 1898 by H. G. Wells, is an example of *invasion literature*, a popular form of *science fiction*. His description of the Martian invasion of earth played on many people's fears about extraterrestrial life, and the belief that something might happen at the turn of the century.

Jane Eyre was written by Charlotte Bronte in 1847. It is a romantic novel, yet also fits into the genre of *gothic horror* due to the lonely setting and the violent actions of the mad woman, Bertha. *The Strange Case of Dr Jekyll and Mr Hyde* fits even more snugly into the gothic horror genre, incorporating mystery, suspense, intrigue and violent murders. The settings incorporate mysterious doors and lonely London streets at night to add to the horror and intrigue. Like *The War of the Worlds, The Strange Case of Dr Jekyll and Mr Hyde* is a novel that explores scientific discovery and exploration.

So, many novels cross between genres and incorporate different elements as the plots unfold. As you study your 19th-century novel for Paper 1, Section B, you will learn to recognize the features of the genre in terms of setting, situations and how characters behave and react.

Looking at the opening of your novel

The opening of a novel is very important in terms of creating intrigue for the reader. Some openings will immediately introduce key themes or characters, whereas others will want to take a wider overview of the novel and make the reader think.

In the opening of *The War of the Worlds,* H. G. Wells creates a strong sense of foreboding.

Source text A

The War of the Worlds by H. G. Wells

No one would have believed, in the last years of the nineteenth century, that human affairs were being watched keenly and closely by intelligences greater than man's and yet as mortal as his own; that as men busied themselves about their affairs they were scrutinized and studied, perhaps almost as narrowly as a man with a microscope might scrutinize the transient creatures that swarm and multiply in a drop of water. With infinite complacency men went to and fro over this globe about their little affairs, serene in their assurance of their empire over matter. It is possible that the infusoria under the microscope do the same. No one gave a thought to the older worlds of space as sources of human danger, or thought of them only to dismiss the idea of life upon them as impossible or improbable. It is curious to recall some of the mental habits of those departed days. At most, terrestrial men fancied there might be other men upon Mars, perhaps inferior to themselves and ready to welcome a missionary enterprise. Yet, across the gulf of space, minds that are to our minds as ours are to those of the beasts that perish, intellects vast and cool and unsympathetic, regarded this earth with envious eyes, and slowly and surely drew their plans against us. And early in the twentieth century came the great disillusionment.

Activity 2

1. Look at the highlighted phrases in the source text opposite and discuss how they present the human race before the Martian invasion. Write single words on sticky notes, to describe how humans are being depicted in this passage. What are the common words?

2. Now look at the way that the Martians are presented in the passage. What do the phrases below tell you? In pairs, write down what each phrase makes you think or feel about the Martians. How are they presented in terms of their attitude to humans?

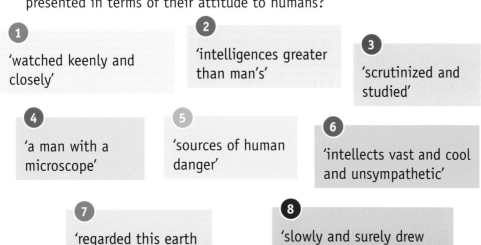

1 'watched keenly and closely'

2 'intelligences greater than man's'

3 'scrutinized and studied'

4 'a man with a microscope'

5 'sources of human danger'

6 'intellects vast and cool and unsympathetic'

7 'regarded this earth with envious eyes'

8 'slowly and surely drew their plans against us'

3. Discuss why this is an effective opening to a science-fiction novel about a Martian invasion of Earth.

In *Pride and Prejudice*, Jane Austen immediately introduces us to the characters of Mr and Mrs Bennet and, through their dialogue, the theme of marriage.

Source text B

Pride and Prejudice by Jane Austen

It is a truth universally acknowledged, that a single man in possession of a good fortune, must be in want of a wife.

However little known the feelings or views of such a man may be on his first entering a neighbourhood, this truth is so well fixed in the minds of the surrounding families, that he is considered as the rightful property of some one or other of their daughters.

'My dear Mr Bennet,' said his lady to him one day, 'have you heard that Netherfield Park is let at last?'

Mr Bennet replied that he had not.

'But it is,' returned she; 'for Mrs Long has just been here, and she told me all about it.'

Mr Bennet made no answer.

'Do you not want to know who has taken it?' cried his wife impatiently.

'*You* want to tell me, and I have no objection to hearing it.'

This was invitation enough.

'Why, my dear, you must know, Mrs Long says that Netherfield is taken by a young man of large fortune from the north of England; that he came down on Monday in a chaise and four to see the place, and was so much delighted with it that he agreed with Mr Morris immediately; that he is to take possession before Michaelmas, and some of his servants are to be in the house by the end of next week.'

Activity 3

1. Look at the opening sentence of the novel and consider whether Jane Austen is telling the truth. If she isn't being truthful, what is she suggesting and why? What central theme has she introduced in the opening sentence of the novel?

2. In this opening to Chapter 1, we are introduced to Mr and Mrs Bennet.

   a. Write down your impressions of Mrs Bennet and explain how you formed these impressions from this extract. Then do the same for Mr Bennet. Look at:

   - what they say

   - how much they say

   - how they respond to what each other says.

   b. Swap your ideas with a partner and compare your impressions. In your pairs, sum up one impression of them as a married couple in a sentence. Write your sentence on a sheet of A3 paper and write your reasons around it.

   c. Now think about their conversation and suggest what it tells you about the importance of marriage in the 19th Century.

3. Now think about the novel you are studying. Look at the opening paragraphs and make notes about what the author is doing. Use the following ideas as a checklist:

Write a paragraph evaluating how successful you think it is as an opening, using the notes you have made.

Focus on narration

Different novels use different forms of narration. Many 19th-century novels use a third-person **narrative** – the voice telling the story is not that of a character involved in the story. Other novels use a first-person narrative – the narrator is a character in the story and conveys the events from his or her perspective. Of course a writer can also use other narrative devices, like a letter or journal entry, so that we view the events from a different perspective at some points in the novel. In some novels we hear the 'authorial voice' very clearly and it can make us react to characters and events in a certain way.

Key term

Narrative an account of events; a story

The Strange Case of Dr Jekyll and Mr Hyde is written in the third person but much of the action is viewed through the eyes of Mr Utterson. In the last two chapters, we are told the events through the words of different characters, firstly Dr Lanyon's narrative in Chapter 9, then finally Henry Jekyll's statement in Chapter 10. These are both narrated in the first person.

Read the following extracts.

Source text C

The Strange Case of Dr Jekyll and Mr Hyde by Robert Louis Stevenson

Chapter 9 – Dr Lanyon's narrative

He put the glass to his lips, and drank at one gulp. A cry followed; he reeled, staggered, clutched at the table and held on, staring with infected eyes, gasping with open mouth; and as I looked, there came, I thought, a change – he seemed to swell – his face became suddenly black, and the features seemed to melt and alter – and the next moment I had sprung to my feet and leaped back against the wall, my arm raised to shield me from that prodigy, my mind submerged in terror.

'O God!' I screamed, and 'O God!' again and again; for there before my eyes – pale and shaken, and half fainting, and groping before him with his hands, like a man restored from death – there stood Henry Jekyll! [...]

Chapter 10 - Henry Jekyll's full statement

When I came to myself at Lanyon's, the horror of my old friend perhaps affected me somewhat: I do not know; it was at least but a drop in the sea to the abhorrence with which I looked back upon these hours. A change had come over me. It was no longer the fear of the gallows, it was the horror of being Hyde that wracked me. I received Lanyon's condemnation partly in a dream; it was partly in a dream that I came home to my own house and got into bed. I slept after the prostration of the day, with a stringent and profound slumber which not even the nightmares that wrung me could avail to break. I awoke in the morning shaken, weakened, but refreshed.

Exam link

In the exam, you will need to show close reading skills and make connections between different parts of the text.

Here we have two perspectives on the same moment in the novel – both characters are looking back on the moment that Dr Lanyon witnessed Jekyll turning back into Hyde and describing how they felt.

Activity 4

1. Look at the extract from Chapter 9. Describe the overall mood and atmosphere of the passage. When you have done this, look back at the passage and highlight the key words and phrases that create this mood and atmosphere.

2. Write a short paragraph explaining how Dr Lanyon reacts to his discovery, using quotations to support your ideas.

3. Now look at the extract from Chapter 10. Does it have the same mood and atmosphere, or a different one? Highlight the key words and phrases in the extract which convey this.

4. Write a paragraph comparing Dr Jekyll's response to this incident to Dr Lanyon's, using quotations to support your ideas. Explain why they react so differently.

5. Show your paragraph to the person sitting next to you. Discuss how the change of narrator helps the reader to understand the characters more deeply.

Activity 5

Find a section of your 19th-century text where the narrative voice is powerful. Highlight or write down the key phrases that show the narrator's feelings most powerfully. What impact do they have on you, as the reader?

You could look at the following sections:

1
Jane Eyre: Jane when she is locked in the red room (Chapter 2)

2
Pride and Prejudice: Elizabeth Bennet when she sees Pemberley for the first time (Chapter 43)

3
The War of the Worlds: The Narrator when he is trapped in the cellar with the Curate (Book 2, Chapter 1)

4
Great Expectations: Young Pip when he first meets Estella and she makes him cry (Chapter 7)

Support

Create a quote bank and list short useful quotes that you have found.

Unit 2 Understanding context

Learning objectives

- To learn to identify contextual elements of your set text
- To use clues in the text to make relevant contextual points
- To write meaningfully about context in exam questions

Key terms

Context the setting or circumstances when a text was written

Setting the location of events

What is context?

In the exam, your answers will need to show an understanding of **context** – the background information about the time in which the novel you are studying was written – which will help you understand the events, themes and characters presented by the writer. Broadly, context can be divided into these areas:

- When the text was written.
- Where the text is set.
- What the society was like at the time the text was written.
- What or who influenced the writer.
- Any political or social influences of the time.

Activity 1

Research the context of your 19th-century set text using the list above. Draw a mind map, like the one that has been started for you below, writing the name of the novel in the centre and adding strands of contextual details that you find out about in your research.

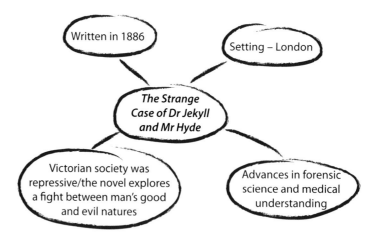

The importance of setting

The **setting** of the novel that you are studying will determine what you need to understand about its historical and social context.

Pride and Prejudice is set in rural England among the upper classes. Jane Austen writes about the world that she knew as a clergyman's daughter. To understand the novel you will need to be aware of the social conventions of the time in which Austen lived:

- a lack of social mobility and strong class consciousness
- a lack of opportunities for women to advance socially other than through marriage.

Source text A

Pride and Prejudice by Jane Austen

... the eye was instantly caught by Pemberley House, situated on the opposite side of a valley into which the road with some abruptness wound. It was a large, handsome stone building, standing well on rising ground, and backed by a ridge of high woody-hills; and in front, a stream of some natural importance was swelled into greater, but without any artificial appearance. Its banks were neither formal nor falsely adorned. Elizabeth was delighted. She had never seen a place for which nature had done more, or where natural beauty had been so little counteracted by an awkward taste. They were all of them warm in their admiration; and at that moment she felt that to be mistress of Pemberley might be something!

Activity 2

Look at the above extract from *Pride and Prejudice* and answer the following questions. When answering these questions, think carefully about the contextual setting of *Pride and Prejudice*.

1. What impression of Pemberley do you get from the description?

2. What does it imply about the person who lives there?

3. What impact does it have on Elizabeth and why?

Activity 3

Choose a significant setting from the novel that you are studying and consider how it is used to develop your understanding of a character or theme.

Here are some suggestions of settings you could look at:

1

Jane Eyre: Jane's view of Thornfield when she returns after the fire. 'I looked with timorous joy towards a stately house; I saw a blackened ruin.'

2

The Strange Case of Dr Jekyll and Mr Hyde: Mr Utterson's description of Dr Jekyll's laboratory. 'It was the first time that the lawyer had been received in that part of his friend's quarters...'

3

The War of the Worlds: The narrator's description of Putney when he returns to London. 'After sunset, I struggled on along the road towards Putney...'

4

Great Expectations: Pip's description of Miss Havisham's dining room. 'I crossed the staircase landing, and entered the room she indicated.'

Tip

Remember to pick very short quotations from the passage to illustrate the points you make.

Using contextual knowledge to inform your understanding

As modern readers, it is important that we understand the differences between our own lives today and how the characters in 19th-century novels would have lived. This allows us to have a much better understanding of the themes of the novels and why they were important at that time.

For example, in the 19th Century the vast majority of people would travel very rarely, even within England. Because people relied on slow forms of transport, like horse-drawn carriages, for most journeys, and roads were very primitive compared to now, even relatively short distances could involve a long and sometimes arduous journey. Communication was also very basic and people relied heavily on letters, which could take a long time to arrive.

The grid opposite has been divided into the different locations Jane Eyre lives at in the novel of the same name. It shows how the events in those locations link to the social and historical context of the novel.

Activity 4

Look at the grid opposite. Write a similar grid for your 19th-century novel, listing the important locations and the key events that happen in them. Research the contextual significance of the key events, using the grid opposite as a guide.

Stretch

Add another column to your grid in which you can add important quotes.

Location	Key events	Contextual significance
Gateshead Hall	Jane is an orphan who is taken in by her aunt, but treated cruelly by her cousins. After standing up for herself she is punished severely and sent away.	In the 19th century, wealth tended to stay in families with the eldest boy inheriting the family estate. Jane is viewed as an 'outsider' and a threat by her cousins and there is little sympathy for her orphaned state, despite being a relation.
Lowood School	A vindictive headmaster makes Jane's life difficult here, but she makes a true friend in Helen Burns and has a kind teacher, Miss Temple. Helen Burns dies and Jane finishes at the school as a teacher.	19th-century schools were very harsh and formal compared to schools today. Great emphasis was placed on moral purity and it was assumed that harsh punishments and humiliation would instil moral behaviour in children. Helen Burns dies of consumption (tuberculosis, as it is known today). Before antibiotics it was far more common for children to die before reaching adulthood.
Thornfield Hall	Jane is appointed as a governess. Mr Rochester, the owner, is seldom there, but when he returns there seems to be an attraction between him and Jane. There are various mysterious happenings, mostly at night.	A governess had a peculiar situation in a household: neither a servant or a member of the family. Jane is treated with respect by Mrs Fairfax and Rochester, but is very awkward when invited to any social functions as she does not fit in.
Gateshead Hall	Jane returns as a much wiser person when her aunt is ill. She discovers that a letter had been sent to her aunt three years earlier from an uncle wanting to adopt her and bequeath her his estate upon his death. Her aunt replied telling him that Jane was dead.	In the 19th century, methods of communication were basic and slow. If a letter did not reach its intended recipient, the consequences could be grave. Because communication was so basic, family deaths and other news would not always be common knowledge to distant relatives.
Thornfield Hall	Rochester and Jane plan to marry but she finds out about his 'wife' Bertha, who is mad and responsible for the mysterious incidents at night. Jane leaves.	Rochester could not divorce Bertha, despite having been tricked into marrying her abroad. Therefore, even though she is insane, he is unable to marry again.
Moor House	Jane is taken in by a kindly brother and sister (who turn out to be her cousins). Jane learns that she has inherited a fortune, which she shares with her cousins. St John proposes to her but she refuses him because he does not love her and she does not love him.	Jane's cousins are living in genteel poverty as their father lost the family wealth. In the 19th century, there were varying reasons for marriage – it was often used to secure wealth, or join powerful families. St John plans to go to India as a missionary and thinks Jane would be a perfect missionary wife. He thinks marriage should be based on practical considerations rather than love. Jane disagrees.
Ferndean	Jane returns to Thornfield to find that Bertha has burnt it down, dying in the fire and blinding Rochester. Jane marries Rochester and they eventually have a son. Rochester's sight returns.	Rochester has waited for Jane, staying as close to the burned-out Thornfield Hall as possible. When Jane returns she is not affected by his disabilities or scars and agrees to marry him as soon as he asks. Jane's position as a financially independent woman changes her, allowing her to make her own decisions.

In *The War of the Worlds*, most of the action takes place in a small area of England.

Read the following extract from an article that was published in *The Guardian* in 2013:

Summer voyages: The War of the Worlds by HG Wells

The narrator's journey is not many miles, but takes him – and the reader – an exhilarating distance from the familiar

A journey doesn't have to be particularly long to change your view of the world. It doesn't even have to take you far from home. In fact, I would argue that one of the most powerful descriptions of a journey in literature works precisely because its narrator stays close to home. Its power comes in showing those familiar places in a new light. Showing them, in fact, in a green-tinged light. And then blowing them to pieces.

Yes, I'm talking about the path of destruction wreaked by the Martians in HG Wells's War of the Worlds. More specifically, I'm thinking of the journey the novel's narrator takes as he battles to survive the invasion. In all, he probably doesn't travel more than 50 miles, and he certainly doesn't leave the beaten path – but that isn't to detract from the profundity of his experience or the epic nature of his struggle. Indeed, it's precisely because he remains in what even now I'm tempted to describe as the "safety" of the Home Counties that The War of the Worlds is so effective. Both because it's disconcerting to see poisonous gas and heat rays laying waste to that comfortable world – and because, it's fun. Who wouldn't want to have a blast at Weybridge, after all?

Certainly HG Wells later claimed to have relished the prospect. In an introduction to a 1920s Atlantic edition of the novel he explained how much he enjoyed cycling around the settings for the novel, diligently noting the outstanding architectural features in each place – and jotting down ideas for how he would wipe them from the map. It's possible even to read the book as an enjoyably mischievous rampage through middle England. Landing the Martians in Woking is certainly a good way to shake commuters out of their bourgeois complacency.

Yet that isn't really how the story comes across, even if Wells may have had a sense of humour, and plenty of interesting thoughts about the morality of late Victorian capitalists. Invasion, he shows carefully and compassionately, is no fun at all. This journey is a nightmare.

Apparently, HG Wells disliked the famous Orson Welles radio broadcast of War of the Worlds because it spread the Martian attack out over too much of the USA. He keeps things deliberately small in scale, for practical tactical reasons (the Martians are able to keep in contact with each other and move on London in formation) and because reporting these intergalactic events on a human scale makes them more vivid and more easy to imagine. After a bit of to-ing and fro-ing to Leatherhead, and a brief visit to Ottershaw Observatory (in whose eminently civilised confines we first meet the narrator, watching the skies and some interesting eruptions on the planet Mars), he travels no further than Kensington – a pleasant day's cycling from Woking. Or a pleasant day's cycling if the Home Counties hadn't just been ravaged by tripod fighting machines and poison gas.

There's still a certain cosiness to the places the narrator visits, which Wells exploits to the full. How strange to read "Byfleet was in a tumult". How odd to think of the waters of the Thames boiling and steaming around the ferry at Shepperton. How unsettling to witness mankind on its knees at Walton-on-Thames, and a soot-smudged curate ranting: "Fire, earthquake death. As if it were Sodom and Gomorrah! All our work undone, all the work –"

The narrator travels by slowly, by pony and trap, by rowing boat, by bike and by foot, sheltering in ordinary suburban houses, eating tins of peaches, drinking beer from bottles. Much of what he encounters is small scale, local, everyday. Naturally, that makes the contrast with the ravaged wastelands left by the Martians all the stronger. Even now, more than 100 years after publication it's easy to picture the scene and share the narrator's horror at losing his home. It's eerie too, to think of the silent London he eventually reaches. Then to feel his dazed horror on his return to Woking and to a life returning to an even keel, but for the odd encounter,

like seeing a pony he left for dead on the way out, the body now picked down to the bones.

In those few miles of travelling the narrator has witnessed the end of human civilisation. Or, at least, civilisation as he knew it. He has journeyed from a world with regular trains, newspaper deliveries, friendly astronomers in convenient observatories, dinner parties and policemen, to starvation, chaos and corpses on the road. He has seen what it is to be invaded. [...]

Activity 5

1. Make a list of what the article suggests about why H. G. Wells deliberately set the novel in a small area of England.

2. Make a map of the narrator's journey through the novel, noting the key events that take place at each location.

Using contextual knowledge effectively in your exam responses

Autobiographical influences

Sometimes the writer uses their own life experiences in their novels – this often adds to the richness and authenticity of the character's reflections.

In *Jane Eyre,* Charlotte Brontë draws on her own experiences of being sent to a strict religious boarding school, then working as a teacher and governess herself. In the novel, Jane, as a penniless orphan, is forced to work as a teacher and a governess to support herself. Through the character of Jane, Brontë is able to explore many of the issues faced by young middle-class women who had to work to support themselves within the very limited opportunities afforded to them at that time.

Great Expectations was written in 1860 when social changes were becoming more apparent in England as industry developed and the populations in cities and towns grew. Charles Dickens used his own experience of his father being put in a debtor's prison to explore criminality and the justice system. He uses the character of Magwitch to show that criminals could reform and become good citizens but that the treatment of convicts at the time did not acknowledge that. He uses the character of Pip to explore the theme of self-improvement in a society where there were still rigid class structures but the notion of social mobility was beginning to be a reality.

It is important that you show your understanding of the social and historical context of your novel through integrating it into relevant ideas in your essays. You should never 'bolt on' factual information in your introduction, but should try to include it in your points about the characters or themes.

Activity 6

Compare these two introductions to an essay on *Great Expectations* where the student has been asked to explore Dickens's presentation of Magwitch in the novel.

Student A

Lots of things that happened to Charles Dickens influenced the events and characters in *Great Expectations*. When Charles Dickens was twelve years old his father was put into prison because he couldn't pay his debts. While he was there Dickens was sent to work in a boot-blacking factory. He stayed working at the factory even after his father was released from prison.

The student has focused on Dickens's own life, but has not made any relevant comments on the novel.

Student B

In *Great Expectations* Dickens explores the notion of criminal behaviour by presenting a convict, Magwitch, as a good man. By doing so he challenges the conventions of the time and questions the morality of punishment in 19th-century England, where people were often given harsh prison sentences for petty crimes or being unable to pay their debts.

The student has acknowledged Dickens's interest in the treatment of criminals but has firmly linked the comments to the presentation of Magwitch in the novel.

Activity 7

1. Choose an important theme in the novel you are studying and carry out research to find relevant contextual information about your chosen theme.

2. Now conduct further research to see if there are any autobiographical details that the writer may have drawn on when exploring that theme.

3. Create a mind map, or another diagram, to show your findings.

   Suggested themes:

   - *Pride and Prejudice*: Social hierarchies
   - *The War of the Worlds*: Survival of the fittest
   - *The Strange Case of Dr Jekyll and Mr Hyde*: The duality of human nature
   - *Jane Eyre*: Genteel poverty
   - *Great Expectations*: Social injustice

Unit 3 Exploring meaning

Learning objectives

- To look for meaning
- To explore character and theme
- To make links and connections with the rest of the set text

Knowing the story

Looking for meaning in your set text means exploring beneath the surface of the novel. First, you need to understand the events of your novel and how the plot unfolds. A secure knowledge of the plot will then allow you to deepen your understanding by exploring the characters and **themes**.

19th-century novels often have complex plots that unfold slowly. It is important that you understand the sequence of events in your set text and how they impact upon the characters. To do this, it is helpful to create a set of notes that will remind you of them – they will be useful for your revision before the final exam.

Remember that some key events may take place before the novel begins! You should also note any time lapses and what has happened during that time.

Activity 1

The table below begins to record the key events in *Great Expectations*.

Before the novel begins	Compeyson abandons Miss Havisham on their wedding day.
	Compeyson and Magwitch are found guilty of passing forged notes. Compeyson blames Magwitch, who receives a longer sentence. They both escape on Christmas Eve.
Chapters 1–6	Pip meets Magwitch and helps him.
	Magwitch and Compeyson are recaptured.
Chapters 8–10	Pip's first and subsequent visits to Satis House, where he meets Miss Havisham and Estella. He also has a fight with a 'pale young gentleman'.
	Miss Havisham pays for Pip to become Joe's apprentice.
Chapters 11–13	Mrs Joe is attacked and Biddy arrives to look after her.
Chapters 14–15	Pip is told about his 'expectations' by Jaggers, a London lawyer. He is to move to London to live as a gentleman. Pip assumes the rich person who has sponsored him is Miss Havisham.
Chapters 16–19	Pip moves to London and starts his new life.
	He meets the 'pale young gentleman' (Herbert Pocket) again. This time they are friends and Pip stays with the Pocket family.

Create your own table, continuing the one above to record all the key events in *Great Expectations*, or create your own table for the text you are studying.

Remember that in the 19th-century serialized novels were very popular. *Great Expectations* was written in serial form and published in a weekly publication from December 1860 until August 1861. People used to wait anxiously for the next 'episode' to find out what was going to happen to the characters next. Very similar to you watching your favourite television programmes now! It meant that episodes often finished on cliff-hangers to make the readers come back for more, so it does have a significant impact on the way that the novel is structured.

Activity 2

Make a timeline of events that affect the relationship between two key characters in your 19th-century text, for example:

- Pip's relationship with Joe in *Great Expectations*
- Elizabeth and Darcy in *Pride and Prejudice*
- Jane and Rochester in *Jane Eyre*
- The narrator and the curate in *The War of the Worlds*
- Mr Utterson and Dr Jekyll in *The Strange Case of Dr Jekyll and Mr Hyde*.

Support

Choose a key quotation for each stage of their relationship.

As you can see from your table, the novel you are studying will naturally fall into sections. Some stories are **chronological**, telling events in the order in which they happen, whereas others will use flashbacks or change the narrator to get a different perspective of the events. For example, the brother's story in *The War of the Worlds*, or Dr Jekyll's account at the end of the novel. However the story in your novel is shaped, it will be possible to divide it into sections.

Activity 3

Imagine that your novel is going to be made into a television series. You have been asked to suggest how it could be divided into six or eight episodes.

Using the table that you have completed in Activity 1, write a description of what will happen in each episode of the series.

Support

Give a title to each episode based on chapter headings, or your own titles.

Stretch

Look for a key quotation from the novel to use as the title of each episode.

Key terms

Chronological actions in the order of which they happened

Chronology the sequence of events in which they first occurred

Tip

Knowing the **chronology** of the story will help you in the exam, as you will be able to put the extract into the context of the novel as a whole and make relevant links to other sections of the novel.

Exploring characters

It is important to have an understanding of all the characters in the novel you are studying, both the major and the minor ones. You need to consider their relationships with other characters and how they contribute to the wider novel.

Activity 4

Make a mind map for one of the central characters in your novel, showing their relationships with other characters. Look at the one that has been started for Pip in *Great Expectations* and use it as a guide.

Support

Make a list of key quotations for your character. Keep them short so that you can revise them for the examination.

Stretch

Extend your mind map to show links between the other characters. Look at relationships, misunderstandings and developments throughout the novel.

Estella – Miss Havisham's adopted daughter who has been brought up incapable of loving anyone. Pip falls in love with Estella but she rejects him and marries Drummle.

Joe – Pip's brother-in-law, who teaches him that being a gentleman is less to do with wealth and class and more to do with kindness and moral behaviour.

Miss Havisham – a bitter old lady who Pip mistakenly thinks is his benefactor, but later finds out that she has used him cruelly in revenge for being rejected on her wedding day.

Pip

Jaggers – the lawyer who Pip deals with when he goes to London to become a gentleman. Jaggers knows that Magwitch is Pip's benefactor, but Pip thinks it is Miss Havisham.

Magwitch – a convict who Pip helps as a young boy in the marshes. He remembers Pip's kindness and becomes his benefactor, allowing Pip to go to London and live as a gentleman.

Herbert Pocket – Pip first meets Herbert at Miss Havisham's house and punches him. They later meet in London and become great friends.

Activity 5

In *The War of the Worlds,* most of the key characters are not given names but given titles. Less important characters, who generally appear in the novel for a short period of time, tend to be named.

Think about why H. G. Wells decided not to name the characters. What effect does this have on the reader?

The key characters are:

- the narrator
- the narrator's wife
- the artilleryman
- the narrator's brother
- the curate.

Activity 6

1. Pick one of the key characters from *The War of the Worlds*. Analyse the character and his or her function in the novel. As they are not named, think about what group of people they might represent in terms of their attitudes, behaviour and response to the Martian invasion.

2. Look at the character chronologically in the novel and note any changes in their behaviour. If they do not appear in the novel at times, explain where they are when they are absent, as this could explain changes in their character or behaviour and attitudes later.

3. Share your ideas with a group. Design a wall chart showing your findings and include quotes to explain your points.

Exploring themes

The themes of a novel require you to explore beyond the explicit text of the story. What does the writer want you to think about? It is likely that the novel you are studying will have several themes.

Activity 7

1. Working with a partner, think about the novel that you are studying and write down all the possible themes that you can think of. Do this as a brainstorming session – just write them all down on a large piece of paper; do not discuss them at this point.

2. When you have done this, draw lines between any themes that you think are closely linked to one another.

3. Prioritise your chosen themes, starting with the one that you think is most important and working down to the one you think is least important.

4. There are some examples of themes from the set texts below. Decide whether these themes are explored in your novel and find evidence to support this. Add them to your list of themes.

Education
Marriage Science
Deceit Love Good and evil
Conflict
Fate Friendship
Growing up Family Social class
Punishment Money

When you have ranked your themes in order, put them into a table and select chapters of your novel where you think they are explored. Put some key quotes in a third column that link to the theme. This will allow you to think about thematic links between different parts of your novel.

Look at the table below that has been started based on *The Strange Case of Dr Jekyll and Mr Hyde*.

Theme	Chapter	Event	Quotes
Conflict and violence	Chapter 1	Enfield's description of the child being trampled	'the man trampled calmly over the child's body' 'it was like some damned Juggernaut'
	Chapter 4	The murder of Carew	'he broke out in a great flame of anger' 'with ape-like fury' 'hailing down a storm of blows' 'there lay his victim... incredibly mangled'

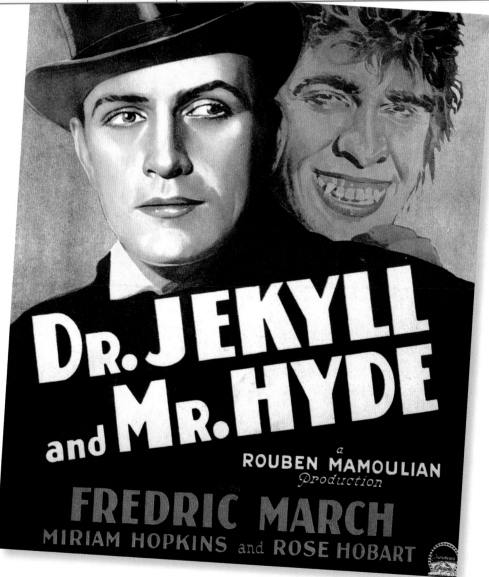

Unit 4 Analysing language

Learning objectives

- To learn to analyse features of language
- To explore the narrative voice
- To learn how to write about the effects of language in the exam, using appropriate subject terminology

Analysing language in a given extract

In your exam response, you must show understanding of the way that the writer of your novel uses language and structure for deliberate effect. This will also involve using appropriate terminology to identify features of language and narration in the novel you are studying.

In the exam, you will be given the option of an extract-based question. Learning to look for language features in the extract given will help you address this assessment objective in your response, although you will have to refer to another part of the novel too.

Look at how this extract from *The War of the Worlds* has been annotated, highlighting language and its effects. Focus on how the writer has created a sense of fear and chaos.

Key term

Metaphor when a writer describes something as if it is something else

A **metaphor** which creates a sense of activity, moving forward in a surge, but also links to the heat.

Emphasizes the huge number of people – 'torrent' dehumanizes them and makes them one mass.

Source text A

The War of the Worlds by H. G. Wells

For the main road was a boiling stream of people, a torrent of human beings rushing northward, one pressing on another. A great bank of dust, white and luminous in the blaze of the sun, made everything within twenty feet of the ground grey and indistinct, and was perpetually renewed by the hurrying feet of a dense crowd of horses and men and women on foot, and by the wheels of vehicles of every description.

'Way!' my brother heard voices crying. 'Make way!'

It was like riding into the smoke of a fire to approach the meeting-point of the lane and the road; the crowd roared like a fire, and the dust was hot and pungent. And, indeed, a little way up the road a villa was burning and sending rolling masses of black smoke across the road to add to the confusions.

It makes the heat seem colourless in its intensity.

Evokes a sense of panic through pushing.

The word 'blaze' makes the sun sound fierce and hostile.

Evokes a sense of fear as the crowd seems to be moving towards further danger, not escaping it. It also has a sense of apocalyptic doom, as though the world is ending.

The black smoke crossing the road adds to the sense of chaos and confusion and indicates that there is nowhere for the crowd to run to. It appeals to our visual sense.

The word 'pungent' appeals to our sense of smell – it makes the dust and smoke seem suffocating and dangerous.

Aural imagery evoking the sound of the people and directly linking them to the flames.

Now look at the below extract from *Pride and Prejudice*. The focus here is on how Austen's use of the narrative voice deliberately affects the way that the reader responds to Mrs Bennet at the supper table at the Netherfield Ball.

Source text B

Pride and Prejudice by Jane Austen

[...] her mother was talking to that one person (Lady Lucas) freely, openly, and of nothing else but of her expectation that Jane would soon be married to Mr Bingley. – It was an animating subject, and Mrs Bennet seemed incapable of fatigue while enumerating the advantages of the match. His being such a charming young man, and so rich, and living but three miles from them were the first points of self-congratulation; and then it was such a comfort to think how fond the two sisters were of Jane, and to be certain that they must desire the connection as much as she could do. It was, moreover, such a promising thing for her younger daughters, as Jane's marrying so greatly must throw them in the way of other rich men; and lastly, it was so pleasant at her time of life to be able to consign her single daughters to the care of their sister, that she might not be obliged to go into company more than she liked. It was necessary to make this circumstance a matter of pleasure, because on such occasions it is the etiquette; but no one was less likely than Mrs Bennet to find comfort in staying at home at any period of her life. She concluded with many good wishes that Lady Lucas might soon be equally fortunate, though evidently and triumphantly believing there was no chance of it.

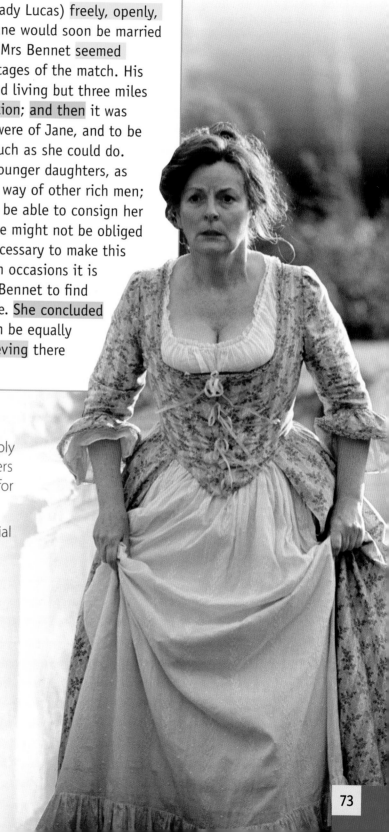

Comment on the yellow highlighted phrases. These phrases stress how much Mrs Bennet is talking and imply that she is being loud and indiscreet, not allowing others to converse. The language is deliberately exaggerated for effect.

Comment on the pink highlighted phrases. The authorial voice intervenes in these phrases with a mocking tone that passes judgement on Mrs Bennet and makes her seem shallow and silly to the reader.

Comment on the orange highlighted phrases. The way that the conversation is narrated indirectly as a list makes Mrs Bennet sound foolish, as though she is chattering away. It allows the authorial voice to intervene and sway the reader's reaction more powerfully than if the conversation had been included in direct speech.

Key terms

Simile when a writer describes something as if it is *like* something else

Personification when a writer gives an inhuman thing human qualities, for example, 'The tree waved its arms in the wind'

Using subject terminology appropriately

You will be expected to use literary terminology in your responses, but just spotting features is not enough. Recognizing literary devices such as **similes**, metaphors and **personification** is essential, but you also need to show that you understand why the writer has used them, their intended effect on the reader.

Look at the exam-style question below, the extract from *The Strange Case of Dr Jekyll and Mr Hyde*, then the sample student answer that follows it.

> How does Stevenson use language to create a sense of horror in this extract and elsewhere in the novel?
>
> [40]

Source text C

The Strange Case of Dr Jekyll and Mr Hyde by Robert Louis Stevenson

"I was coming home from some place at the end of the world, about three o'clock of a black winter morning, and my way lay through a part of town where there was literally nothing to be seen but lamps. Street after street, and all the folks asleep – street after street, all lighted up as if for a procession, and all as empty as a church – till at last I got into that state of mind when a man listens and listens and begins to long for the sight of a policeman. All at once, I saw two figures: one a little man who was stumping along eastward at a good walk, and the other a girl of maybe eight or ten who was running as hard as she was able down a cross-street. Well, sir, the two ran into one another naturally enough at the corner; and then came the horrible part of the thing; for the man trampled calmly over the child's body and left her screaming on the ground. It sounds nothing to hear, but it was hellish to see. It wasn't like a man; it was like some damned Juggernaut."

Student A

In this extract, Stevenson creates a sense of horror by using lots of metaphors and other techniques. For example, 'a black winter morning' is a metaphor because a morning can't really be black. This has an effect on the reader and makes them want to read on. The street is described using a simile 'as empty as a church', which shows us that the streets are empty. There is an oxymoron used when he says 'trampled calmly' because the words trampled and calmly can't really go together. This is because if you are trampling something it sounds as though you are not being calm. This is very effective for the reader. There is also another metaphor used when the man is described as a 'damned Juggernaut' because he isn't really a juggernaut, he is just behaving like one.

Link your response to the question to make sure you are focused.

What is the effect of describing a morning as 'black'? Think of the key word in the question – 'horror'.

Avoid making general statements as they don't show any understanding of that specific text.

Student A's response (page 74) shows you that being able to recognize literary devices and explain what they are is not an effective use of subject terminology. You need to go further and show that you really understand how they are effective. This may be in terms of building atmosphere, creating humour or developing a character. Now read Student A's response, after receiving the teacher's feedback, below:

Student A

In this extract, Stevenson creates a sense of horror through his use of language to depict a horrific and shocking scene. The metaphor 'a black winter morning' immediately shows us that it is dark and gloomy and sets the scene for something horrific to happen. The street is described using a simile 'as empty as a church', which builds up suspense by creating a scene of loneliness and isolation. Enfield himself is nervous, which is shown in the repetition of 'listens and listens' as he longs for a policeman to appear and make him feel safe. When the man and the child collide on a corner we are told that the man 'trampled calmly' over the child. This oxymoron is shocking because it sounds as though he doesn't care about hurting her, despite the obvious violence of his movement in 'trampled'. This image of violence is continued when he is described as a 'damned Juggernaut', as though he is an unstoppable force as he stamps on an innocent child.

> What is the effect of the 'empty streets' in terms of creating atmosphere? Think of 'horror'.

> What does the oxymoron tell us about Mr Hyde's attitude to hurting the girl? What effect does that have?

> What does behaving like a 'Juggernaut' tell us about Mr Hyde and why is that shocking? What does juggernaut mean in Jekyll and Hyde?

Activity 1

Choose an extract from the novel that you are studying. Select a focus point such as character development, creation of atmosphere or evoking a deliberate reader response.

1. Highlight all the interesting words and phrases in the extract.

2. Using these words and phrases, list the literary devices you can find in the extract and find an appropriate quote to support each one.

3. Write a sentence for each quote. In the sentence, you must incorporate the quote (so keep them short!), explain the effect of the literary device and define it. Make sure you keep focused on the question in each sentence.

4. Now use your sentences to write up a paragraph answering the question on your chosen extract. You may need to rewrite some of the sentences so that you don't repeat yourself and to make it as fluent as possible.

Stretch

Now choose two further moments in the novel that link to your extract in theme or subject and repeat the steps above.

Tip

You will have about 50 minutes to respond to the extract and make links to other moments in the text. Spend about 25 minutes on the extract. Use the extract to comment on language (AO2), using short quotations.

Unit 5 Making links and connections

Learning objectives

- To learn how to respond to an extract-based question
- To learn how to link exam extracts to other relevant part of the texts effectively
- To learn to use the question and extract for clues

Linking to other parts of the novel

In the extract-based question on the 19th-century novel you are studying, you will be expected to write about the extract in detail, but also show understanding of the wider text by making links to other parts of the novel.

You must read the question carefully to make sure that you understand its focus, as this will help you decide which sections of the novel to look at.

Activity 1

Look at the following sample exam questions and work out what the focus of each question is.

The following are extract-based questions. Look at the first example; the focus of the question is in italics. This has been highlighted to show quotes that could be used in your answer and notes to help plan a response. They focus on AO2, as using the extract to make lots of AO2 points is helpful in the extract-based question.

Explore how Wells presents ideas about *what makes an enemy dangerous and terrifying*, in this extract and elsewhere in the novel.

[40]

How does Brontë present people being treated unfairly here and elsewhere in the novel?

[40]

You also have the option of a discursive essay question. You are not given an extract for these questions and can choose which parts of the novel to refer to in your answer. You still need to understand the focus of the question and must refer to at least two different sections of the novel to demonstrate understanding of the whole text. Here are examples of discursive exam questions.

How does Dickens present Pip learning lessons the hard way in at least two moments from the novel?

[40]

'Mr Bennet is a lazy father who takes no real interest in his daughters.' Referring to at least two moments in the novel, how far would you agree with this view?

[40]

Tip

Remember that as this is a 'closed book' exam you will need to have learned quotes to support your points.

Tip

Remember to make lots of language points on the extract to address AO2.

Tip

Remember that you must show awareness of the cultural context to address AO3.

Source text A

The War of the Worlds by H. G. Wells

In this extract, the Martians return.

Then suddenly we saw a rush of smoke far away up the river, a puff of smoke that jerked up into the air, and hung, and forthwith the ground heaved underfoot and a heavy explosion shook the air, smashing two or three windows in the houses near, and leaving us astonished.

'Here they are!' shouted a man in a blue jersey. 'Yonder! D'yer see them? Yonder!'

Quickly, one after the other, one, two, three, four of the armoured Martians appeared, far away over the little trees, across the flat meadows that stretch towards Chertsey, and striding hurriedly towards the river. Little cowled figures they seemed at first, going with a rolling motion and as fast as flying birds.

Then, advancing obliquely towards us, came a fifth. Their armoured bodies glittered in the sun, as they swept swiftly forward upon the guns, growing rapidly larger as they drew nearer. One on the extreme left, the remotest, that is, flourished a huge case high in the air, and the ghostly terrible Heat-Ray I had already seen on Friday night smote towards Chertsey, and struck the town.

At sight of these strange, swift and terrible creatures, the crowd along the water's edge seemed to me to be for a moment horror-struck. There was no screaming or shouting, but a silence. Then a hoarse murmur and a movement of feet – a splashing from the water. A man, too frightened to drop the portmanteau he carried on his shoulder, swung around and sent me staggering with a blow from the corner of his burden. A woman thrust at me with her hand and rushed past me. I turned too, with the rush of the people, but I was not too terrified for thought. The terrible Heat-Ray was in my mind. To get under water! That was it!

Creates a sense of distance, that the enemy is within reach but can't yet be seen. Builds up tension and fear.

Stresses the might of the enemy, the ground is vibrating with the weight of the advance.

An explosion is aggressive. They are under attack from an enemy they can't see yet.

He is not a soldier, just an ordinary man, which makes him sound vulnerable.

The way that the narrator counts them as they appear reflects what he can see – they are faced with a terrifying enemy and the numbers are unknown.

The speed of the Martian advance is stressed. The people are no match for them.

Military language describes them as an army.

It doesn't seem real.

Attacking language.

The final paragraph of the extract describes for the first time the reaction of the crowd.

A sense of stunned shock and disbelief. Absolute terror.

The narrator builds up the crowd's reactions and zooms in on individuals.

Emphasizes the mass panic and mob mentality.

Both hurt others in their desire to escape, which indicates panic, confusion and survival of the fittest.

The narrator thinks about survival and protecting himself.

Once you have annotated the extract, you need to think about other parts of the novel where similar ideas are explored. Do not try to do too much, as you cannot write about the whole novel. Try to think of at least two relevant parts though. The ideas here to explore are:

- the appearance and behaviour of the 'enemy'
- the reactions – of crowds and individuals
- the sense of war/invasion created through the language.

Earlier parts of the novel that could be linked to this one include:

- the opening of the cylinder and the first sight of a Martian in Chapter 4
- the first use of the Heat-Ray in Chapter 5
- the narrator's first sight of the tripod in Chapter 10
- the artilleryman's description of the battle on the common in Chapter 11.

Later parts include:

- the use of the black smoke in Chapter 15
- the crowd fleeing London in Chapter 16
- the Thunder Child fighting back in Chapter 17.

Before choosing the other parts of the text to link to, think about the ideas being explored in the extract and how those moments fit into them. One of your links may focus on the appearance and behaviour of the Martians, whereas one may focus more on the reactions of the crowd and individuals. Whether your links come before or after the extract may be significant too.

Tip

You need to know your 19th-century novel to be able to make links and connections between different parts of the text. You will also need to be able to place the extract you are given in the context of the novel as a whole.

Activity 2

Choose a key theme from the novel you are studying.

1. Create a mind map of all the moments in the novel when your theme is explored.
2. Link different moments to each other through the characters or the ideas being used to explore the theme.

On pages 77, 79 and 80 are extracts from the 19th-century novels in the exam. You should use your set text extract to start you off.

Support	**Stretch**
Start with the major theme of your text and choose the key moments for your mapping document.	Add quotes to support your ideas.

Source text B

The Strange Case of Dr Jekyll and Mr Hyde by Robert Louis Stevenson

'He is not easy to describe. There is something wrong with his appearance; something displeasing, something downright detestable. I never saw a man I so disliked, and yet I scarce know why. He must be deformed somewhere; he gives a strong sense of deformity, although I couldn't specify the point. He's an extraordinary-looking man, and yet I really can name nothing out of the way. No, sir; I can make no hand of it; I can't describe him. And it's not want of memory; for I declare I can see him this moment.'

> Mr Hyde as the embodiment of evil.

Source text C

Jane Eyre by Charlotte Brontë

Reader, I married him. A quiet wedding we had: he and I, the parson and the clerk, were alone present. When we got back from church, I went into the kitchen of the manor-house, where Mary was cooking the dinner, and John cleaning the knives, and I said –

'Mary, I have been married to Mr Rochester this morning.' The housekeeper and her husband were both of that decent, phlegmatic order of people, to whom one may at any time safely communicate a remarkable piece of news without incurring the danger of having one's ears pierced by some shrill ejaculation, and subsequently stunned by a torrent of wordy wonderment. Mary did look up, and she did stare at me; the ladle with which she was basting a pair of chickens roasting at the fire, did for some three minutes hang suspended in air, and for the same space of time John's knives also had rest from the polishing process; but Mary, bending over the roast, said only –

'Have you, miss? Well, for sure!'

> Jane and Rochester's relationship.

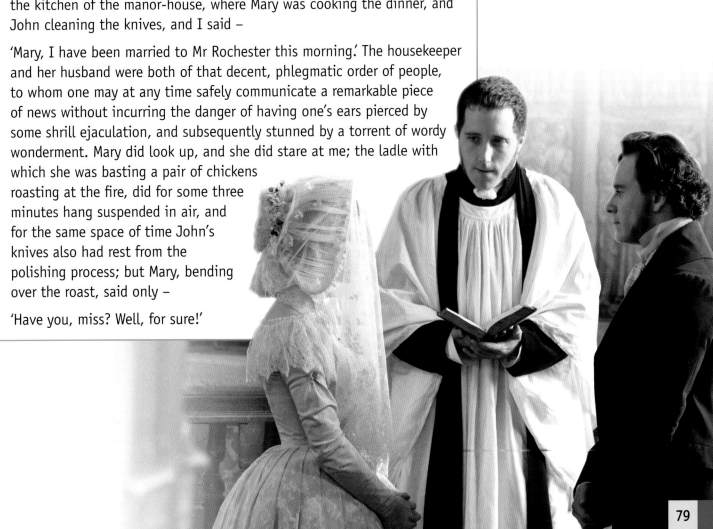

Source text D

Pride and Prejudice by Jane Austen

Having now a good house and a very sufficient income, he intended to marry; and in seeking a reconciliation with the Longbourn family he had a wife in view, as he meant to choose one of the daughters, if he found them as handsome and amiable as they were represented by common report. This was his plan of amends – of atonement – for inheriting their father's estate; and he thought it an excellent one, full of eligibility and suitableness, and excessively generous and disinterested on his part.

His plan did not vary on seeing them. – Miss Bennet's lovely face confirmed his views, and established all his strictest notions of what was due to seniority; and for the first evening she was his settled choice.

> Theme of marriage in the novel.

Source text E

Great Expectations by Charles Dickens

I was to leave our village at five in the morning, carrying my little hand-portmanteau, and I had told Joe that I wished to walk away all alone. I am afraid – sore afraid – that this purpose originated in my sense of the contrast there would be between me and Joe, if we went to the coach together. I had pretended with myself that there was nothing of this taint in the arrangement; but when I went up to my little room on this last night, I felt compelled to admit that it might be so, and had an impulse upon me to go down again and entreat Joe to walk with me in the morning. I did not.

> Social class in the novel.

Activity 3

1. Once you have completed Activity 2, try to turn your theme and extract into an exam-style question:

> How does (*author's name*) present (*theme chosen*) here and elsewhere in the novel?

2. Use your mind map to write a plan for your response.

3. Now write the introduction to your response, which should make some comment about the extract and also explain what other moments in the novel you intend to discuss.

4. Swap your introduction with a partner. Read one another's work and offer ideas for improvement.

Stretch

Write the full response, making sure that you refer to at least two moments from the text in addition to the extract.

Unit 6 Getting ready for the exam

Learning objectives

- To understand the questions and plan a response
- To use quotes and textual references effectively
- To write introductions and conclusions to a response

Tip

When revising, don't learn long quotations. Concentrate instead on short, precise quotations for each character and theme so that you can comment in detail on their language and its effect.

The exam questions

You only have 45 minutes to write your response, so your answer cannot cover all aspects of the question. The questions are designed to help you plan a response in the time provided.

There is a choice of two questions on your 19th-century novel. You must choose one question.

You can either:

1. begin with an extract and make links and connections to other parts of the novel, or

2. explore at least two moments from the novel.

You will be assessed on both questions as follows:

Assessment Objective		% of marks
AO1:	**Critical interpretation** and textual support	35%
AO2:	**Language analysis**	35%
AO3:	Understanding of **context**	20%
AO4:	Vocabulary, sentences, spelling and punctuation	10%

In this question, you are assessed on AO4: use a range of vocabulary and sentence structures for clarity, purpose and effect, with accurate spelling and punctuation, with a mark out of 4 given for this.

This means that you must think carefully about *how* you write, as well as *what* you write. There is more to this than spelling and punctuation. You need to use suitable vocabulary and vary your sentences for effect. Simple sentences can make strong points very effectively. Use longer sentences for more complex tasks, such as balancing one viewpoint about a text with another.

If you choose your own moments, they need to help you to:

- address the question, showing *knowledge* of the novel (AO1)
- make references to the text through quotations or close references (AO1)
- develop your own *personal response* (AO1)
- explore the writer's *effects* through analysis of language and imagery (AO2)
- use appropriate *subject terminology* (AO2)
- understand how the *narrative voice/style* can *affect* the reader (AO2)
- appreciate how *context* can *influence your understanding* of the novel (AO3).

Planning your response

Whether you choose to do the extract-based question, or the essay question, you should spend 5 minutes planning your response.

In 45 minutes, you will be able to write about five paragraphs:

☑ an introduction, opening out the implications of the question (1 paragraph)

☑ detailed exploration of two or three key moments from different parts of the novel (3 paragraphs)

☑ and a conclusion, giving your personal response, based on the evidence you have looked at.

Allowing 5 minutes for planning and checking is crucial, as you have only about 8 minutes for each paragraph. Make sure you have plenty of specific things to say about each key moment to attract marks.

Choosing the right question

You may feel more comfortable choosing the extract-based question, as this will allow you to use the printed extract to cover AO2 by looking closely at the way the writer uses language and techniques in the extract for specific effects.

You should read both questions carefully, however, as the essay-based question may be based on a character or theme that you know well.

In the previous unit, we looked at how to approach extract-based questions, making good links to the wider text. We are now going to think about how to approach the essay questions where you have to select your own moments in the novel to discuss.

It is important to get your essay off to a good start. Ensure you don't answer the question yet – save that for your conclusion! Try to open out the implications of the question by:

☑ addressing all three AOs in your first paragraph

☑ giving an overview of the whole text and the character's role or importance of the theme

☑ introducing the key moments you will explore in detail, explaining their significance.

Make sure the spelling and punctuation in that first paragraph make a good first impression.

Activity 1

Look at the sample student introductions to the essay question on *Pride and Prejudice* on page 84.

Using the checklist points above, decide if Student A and Student B have written effective introductions to their responses.

'Mrs Bennet is a bad mother who is responsible for her daughters' problems.' How far do you agree with this view? Explore at least two moments from the novel to support your ideas.

[40]

Student A

Mrs Bennet is almost made a caricature by Jane Austen, and is shown frequently in the novel trying to marry her daughters off to give them a 'secure' life. However, a lot of the time she ends up preventing them from doing so because of her outrageous behaviour. Her behaviour at both the Netherfield Ball and at Mr Bingley's estate (after forcing Jane to travel in the rain and become ill) encourages Mr Darcy and the Bingley sisters to try to separate Mr Bingley and Jane. By using Elizabeth's reactions – 'mortifying', 'shame', 'mortified' – and the action of Darcy 'silently observing', Austen conveys to the reader how blind Mrs Bennet is to her embarrassing actions and the shame she brings to Jane.

Student B

In *Pride and Prejudice*, Mrs Bennet is a key character whom Austen uses to mock and create irony. She is the mother of Lizzie and her siblings and the wife of their father, Mr Bennet. Austen uses Mrs Bennet to explore the different types of marriages, as well as the way in which marriage is an important concept. The opening of the novel is our first introduction to the Bennets, particularly Mrs Bennet. We immediately understand how important getting her daughters married is: 'The business of her life was to get her daughters married, its solace was visiting and news'.

Activity 2

1. Find the essay question below based on the novel you have studied. Write an introduction, using the checklist on page 83. Before you write your introduction, you will need to decide which moments in the novel you are going to explore by planning your response.

The Strange Case of Dr Jekyll and Mr Hyde

'Mr Utterson's behaviour and attitudes contribute to the suspense in the novel.' How far do you agree with this view? Explore at least two moments from the novel to support your ideas.

[40]

The War of the Worlds

'The Martian invasion brings out the best and the worst in human nature.' How far do you agree with this view? Explore at least two moments from the novel to support your ideas.

[40]

Great Expectations

'Money is the source of all Pip's problems.' How far do you agree with this view? Explore at least two moments from the novel to support your ideas.

[40]

Jane Eyre

'Jane sometimes brings about her own suffering.' How far do you agree with this view? Explore at least two moments from the novel to support your ideas.

[40]

---

2. Now swap your introduction with a partner. Use the checklist to see whether everything has been covered.

3. Look at the moments in the text that have been selected. Compare yours with your partner's and discuss whether some choices are better than others.

4. Look back at your introduction and see whether you can improve it.

If you choose the extract-based question, make sure your introduction refers to the focus of the question, but also that you explain clearly which other moments in the novel you intend to look at in your response. This will ensure that you have planned your response before you begin writing it.

Activity 3

Look at Student A's and Student B's introductions to the extract-based question on *The War of the Worlds* from Unit 5 on page 76-77. Consider which student shows evidence of planning, and knowledge of the wider text, as well as the extract given.

Student A

Wells makes the Martians a dangerous and terrifying enemy throughout the novel, *The War of the Worlds*. In this extract, the humans begin to learn of their full capabilities, as they advance upon them, with Wells using language linked with death to describe 'the ghostly terrible Heat-Ray', foreshadowing the destruction that is yet to come. Their danger is also apparent in other sections of the novel, such as the narrator's first sighting of a Martian close-up in Chapter 4, where he describes it as having 'Gorgon groups of tentacles' and says that he 'was overcome with disgust and dread'. This occurs shortly before he witnesses the Martians' first use of the heat-ray to exterminate the deputation, 'an almost noiseless and blinding flash of light' as he sees 'death leaping from man to man'. Later in the novel, when hiding in the cellar, the narrator has a chance to study the Martians more closely and his terror is palpable as he witnesses the 'ruddy, middle-aged man… three days before he must have been walking the world…' lifted from the cage on the fighting machine's back and consumed by this terrifying enemy.

Student B

Wells presents ideas about what makes an enemy dangerous and terrifying in this extract by describing the reactions of the humans. He writes 'no screaming or shouting, but a silence.' This is followed by 'a man too frightened to drop the portmanteau he carried on his shoulder.' This shows how terrifying the enemy is because they are too frightened to make a noise at first. The weapons they use also show how terrifying and dangerous they are. The heat-ray is described as 'ghostly' and 'terrible' in the extract and builds an image of power which helps you picture the destruction. He also uses personification 'the ground heaved underfoot and a heavy explosion shook the air, smashing two or three of the windows in the house near.' This makes the oblivion caused by the Martians to be greater.

Activity 4

1. Draft more essay questions on characters and themes from your own novel.
2. Practise opening paragraphs.
3. Practise choosing key moments to illustrate your points.
4. Choose interesting examples of language to support your arguments with analysis of the writer's effects.
5. Practise drawing up conclusions.

Progress check

Use this table to check how well you understand your 19th-century novel, and how confident you are that you can write an exam response which meets the assessment objectives.

	I still have some questions about this	I am sure I understand this	I am confident I can give clear explanations with examples
I understand the contextual differences between 19th-century and present-day literature.			
I know the story of my novel and the order in which the events happen.			
I understand the main themes of my novel.			
I understand the characters and their role and purpose in the novel.			
I can appreciate the effect of the narrative voice.			
I can explain some of the language used for specific effects on the reader in extracts from my novel.			
I can see why the themes of my novel are so important.			
I can understand why different audiences react to characters in different ways.			
I can confidently express my personal response based on evidence.			
I have learned enough quotations on the characters and themes of my novel.			
I can use quotations effectively to support the points I make in my essays.			
I can sustain a critical style, and use a range of vocabulary and sentence structures accurately.			

3 Poetry

Component Overview

- You will study one poetry cluster from your anthology and prepare to answer one question (split into two parts) in Section A of Paper 2: Exploring poetry and Shakespeare.

- You will answer both parts of the question on the poetry cluster *you have studied*. These two parts are worth 20 marks each, and together are worth 25% of your total GCSE mark.

- The first part to your question, Part A, will ask you to compare a poem you have studied with an *unseen poem*.

- The second part, Part B, will ask you to explore a poem of your choice from your cluster *in detail* and relate it to the question asked in Part A.

- The mark scheme for this exam divides marks between the Assessment Objectives as follows:

Assessment Objective	Part A: Comparing a seen and unseen extract	Part B: Exploring another poem in your cluster
AO1: Critical interpretation and textual support	40%	50%
AO2: Language analysis	60%	50%
AO3: Understanding of context	Not assessed	Not assessed

Set texts

You need to study one cluster in the 'The OCR Poetry Anthology: Towards a World Unknown'. There are 45 poems in the Anthology, divided equally into the three clusters:

Love and Relationships (15 poems)

Conflict (15 poems)

Youth and Age (15 poems)

As you will also be looking at an unseen poem in Part A of the exam question it's a really good idea to read and think about the poems in the other two clusters too. This will help you get used to reading and responding to poems that you haven't studied in detail.

Activity

1. Create a grid for yourselves like the one below, with spaces for each of the fifteen poems in your cluster, and add to it each time you study one of the poems in your cluster. The first poem in each of the clusters has been included as an example.

Anthology cluster	Name of poem and poet	How poem relates to theme of the cluster	Key quotations
Love and Relationships	*A Song* Helen Maria Williams	It is a love poem spoken by a woman. She is separated from her loved one and this has created anxiety and fear about their relationship.	'He gave me all his heart' 'When love is all I prize' 'Alas! At every breeze I weep – The storm is in my soul'
Conflict	*A Poison Tree* William Blake	This is an abstract rather than personal poem that considers the consequences of anger and conflict. Anger ('wrath') feeds on itself and creates destruction.	'I was angry with my foe: I told it not, my wrath did grow' 'And it grew both day and night Till it bore an apple bright' 'In the morning glad I see My foe outstretched beneath the tree'
Youth and Age	*Holy Thursday* William Blake	Poem presents a picture of childhood innocence and purity. These are poor children who the speaker advises should be cherished.	'O what a multitude they seem'd these flowers of London town' 'Thousands of little boys & girls raising their innocent hands' 'Then cherish pity; lest you drive an angel from your door'

Unit 1 How do you study poetry?

Why does poetry matter?

People were composing, performing, listening to and sharing poems long before they were writing them down. Telling stories through poetry and lyrics is a very important part of our culture and has been for hundreds of years. From nursery rhymes that parents tell their children to the verses that appear on gravestones to commemorate someone's life, poetry describes and surrounds us. What do we do to calm a crying baby? We rock them and perform nursery rhymes and lullabies to soothe them. When we go to primary school, we chant and perform rhymes in the playground. When we are teenagers, many of us learn by heart the lyrics of pop songs. And later in our lives, when we are trying to express some of our most heartfelt emotions, such as love and loss, we turn to verse to convey our feelings.

Activity 1

What can you remember about the verses and poetry of your childhood?

1. Make a list of any poems, nursery rhymes or verses you can remember hearing when you were younger. Try to also think about where you heard these poems. At home, or at nursery, on television, in a computer game?

2. Can you remember any chants, rhyming games or verses from primary school? Think about playtime as well as in class. Jot down what you remember.

3. Can you remember the first song that you knew all of the lyrics to?

4. Share your answers with a partner. What similarities and differences are there in what you have come up with?

Why study poetry?

Poets use language to create pictures, or images, in the mind of the reader or listener but it can be difficult to visualize the world that the poet is drawing, especially if that world is different to our own. Some of the poems you are studying are from the 18th and 19th centuries and the images can feel remote. We also arrive at these images through what can seem like challenging language. But the more you study and read poetry, the more will be revealed.

Look at the painting opposite. It is called *The Lady of Shalott* by John Williams Waterhouse and was painted in 1888. It illustrates part of a famous poem of the same name by Alfred, Lord Tennyson.

'The Lady of Shalott' by Alfred, Lord Tennyson is a **ballad**. The poem tells the legend of a lady trapped in a tower. She can only watch the world outside through a mirror and must weave what she sees into a tapestry. One day she looks straight out through the window, the mirror cracks and she decides to leave her tower.

Key term

Ballad a form of verse or narrative often set to music

Activity 2

1. Look at the painting above for about 10 seconds before covering it up. Jot down the things you remember seeing in the picture. Share these observations with a partner.

2. Now look again, this time for a few minutes, studying the painting as closely as you can. What are the most important things you missed the first time?

3. Perhaps these observations have thrown up more questions than answers. What could be the 'story' behind this poem? Why is this woman in the boat? Why is she dressed as she is? What do you think her mood is? Write a short descriptive passage to sum up your ideas.

Glossary

seer a person of supposed supernatural insight who sees visions of the future

Camelot the place where King Arthur held his court

Source text A

'The Lady of Shalott' by Alfred, Lord Tennyson

With a steady stony glance—

Like some bold **seer** in a trance,

Beholding all his own mischance,

Mute, with a glassy countenance—

    She look'd down to **Camelot**.

It was the closing of the day:

She loos'd the chain, and down she lay;

The broad stream bore her far away,

    The Lady of Shalott.

Activity 3

Read the **stanza** on the left from the poem, 'The Lady of Shalott'.

1. Some of the words have been explained but, once you have read the extract, try to work out any of the other words that you might not be familiar with, or look them up in a dictionary.

2. How well do you think John Williams Waterhouse represents this stanza in his painting?

How to read poetry

There are lots of strategies that you can use to help you read poems, both the poems in your OCR Poetry Anthology and the unseen poems you will also have to comment on.

A good starting point is to get involved with the poem by reading it with a pencil in your hand. Be an active reader, underlining key words, marking difficult words or ideas, drawing arrows between parts with shared meanings, making brief comments on what you think the poem is about. The annotations on the poem opposite give some examples of the kinds of things you could make notes on while reading.

Tip

When you are making annotations, be sure to link them to the points you want to make. Don't just spot the features.

Key terms

Formal language
language that has strict grammatical structures and generally uses standard or technical vocabulary

Archaic language
words that are no longer used in everyday language and have lost a particular meaning

Figurative language
language used to describe by comparing it to something else, using words not to be taken literally, such as in metaphors and similes

Metaphor when a writer describes something as if it *is* something else

Simile when a writer describes something as if it is *like* something else

Activity 4

1. Read the poem opposite aloud or listen to it being read. Poems are designed to be performed and the rhythms of the language will be much more apparent out loud. This can really help with your understanding.

Activity 5

Here is a checklist of ways of responding to an unseen poem. Add your own ideas to the ones already listed below.

1. Think about the subject of the poem and consider the following:

   a. The title. What associations does the title have for you? What does it suggest the poem might be about?

   The voice of a child? A particular year of childhood?

   b. The situation. What seems to be going on? Who is talking? What are the circumstances in which the poem takes place?

   An adult's memory of primary school. The details are precise. Everything seems happy at the start but becomes threatening as it progresses.

   c. The attitude. What can we say about the tone of voice of the narrator of the poem? Is it happy, sad, humorous or regretful, for example?

   Seems quite a joyful and nostalgic tone at the start but the tone later becomes rather more impatient and anxious.

2. Think about the language of the poem. Is it written in everyday language? Or **formal language**? Or **archaic language**? Do you notice any repetitions or patterns of language in the poem? How about **figurative language** like **metaphors** or **similes**?

Stretch

Duffy uses words that evoke the senses: smell, taste, touch, sound and sight. Find some examples of each. Why do you think Duffy has chosen to use these words? What effect do they have?

Source text B

'In Mrs Tilscher's Class'
by Carol Ann Duffy

You could travel up the Blue Nile
with your finger, tracing the route
while Mrs Tilscher chanted the scenery.
'Tana. Ethiopia. Khartoum. Aswan.'
That for an hour, then a skittle of milk
and the chalky Pyramids rubbed into dust.
A window opened with a long pole.
The laugh of a bell swung by a running child.

This was better than home. Enthralling books.
The classroom glowed like a sweetshop.
Sugar paper. Coloured shapes. Brady and Hindley
faded, like the faint, uneasy smudge of a mistake.
Mrs Tilscher loved you. Some mornings, you found
she'd left a gold star by your name.
The scent of a pencil slowly, carefully, shaved.
A xylophone's nonsense heard from another form.

Over the Easter term the inky tadpoles changed
from commas into exclamation marks. Three frogs
hopped in the playground, freed by a dunce,
followed by a line of kids, jumping and croaking
away from the lunch queue. A rough boy
told you how you were born. You kicked him, but stared
at your parents, appalled, when you got back home.

That feverish July, the air tasted of electricity.
A tangible alarm made you always untidy, hot,
fractious under the heavy, sexy sky. You asked her
how you were born and Mrs Tilscher smiled,
then turned away. Reports were handed out.
You ran through the gates, impatient to be grown,
as the sky split open into a thunderstorm.

Seems like the voice of a child.

Use of the second person form of address. Makes it everybody's experience.

Speaker doesn't know or doesn't want to use Mrs Tilscher's first name.

Bottle of milk shaped like a skittle? What might this look like? Why this image?

Feels like an old-fashioned building with high windows.

Unit 2 Understanding the theme: Love and relationships

Learning objectives

- To explore the theme of each of the three clusters and possible meanings or ideas that might be connected

- To focus on the skills of identifying the key themes of the poems in the cluster and to make links to other poems

Thinking about the theme of your cluster

How can we begin to think about the themes and ideas contained in the poems in your cluster? Each of these themes represents something pretty large in human experience, so it figures *we already know* quite a lot about the theme. Perhaps what will be interesting when we study the poems is how what we already know will be reflected, or challenged, by the poems studied?

Activity 1

'Love and relationships' contains two themes.

1. Jot down words and associations you have with each word. For 'love', for example, you might have a **synonym** like 'infatuation', and for 'relationships' you might jot down 'friendship'.

2. Below is a simple Venn diagram to picture the connections between love and relationships. Where the circles overlap is where the two sets have things in common. Copy the diagram on to paper and add some of your thoughts about each word into the circles.

3. Are there words or ideas common to both lists? Copy these into the overlapping section and add any more ideas about how love and relationships combine.

4. Share what you have written with others.

Key term

Synonym a word or phrase that has the same meaning as another word or phrase

Venn diagram

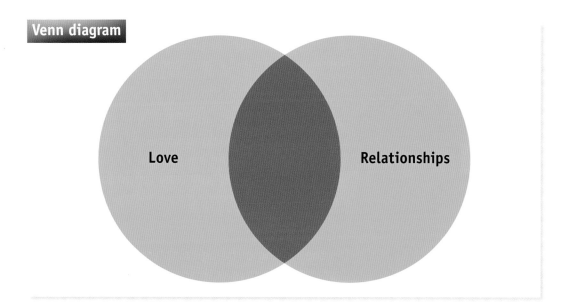

Love   Relationships

The poems in the cluster cover many different attitudes to love and relationships. In the exam, you will be given one poem from the cluster and asked to compare it with another of your choice that has some connections with it. The question might ask you, for example, to think about two poems that deal with unrequited love or the love felt between members of the same family.

Activity 2

1. Below are some examples of the different types of love represented in this cluster. Match each 'love type' to its definition found online at www.urbandictionary.com.

2. What other types of love can you think of?

Love type	Definition
Everlasting love	When you've lost someone that was your world, who meant everything to you. When you lose them you feel empty, hurt and neglected.
Lost love	Can be shown by a handwritten note, by going for a walk, or even by making someone a sandwich. Romance is something simple and sweet that reminds your partner why they fell in love with you in the first place.
Romantic love	It's the feeling of being completely, hopelessly, desperately in love with someone, all the while knowing your feelings will never reach them.
Unrequited love	When you think that the love you have for someone is never-ending or will last until death.

Activity 3

Look at the extracts below from poems in the cluster. Match each quotation to a love type in Activity 2. What clues are there in the language? Write down the quotation and your justification. One example has been completed for you.

Key term

Pathetic fallacy when an author attributes human emotions to aspects of nature, such as 'an angry storm' or 'sullen rocks'

1
'I am trapped in it. I can't move. I want you.' ('Dusting the Phone')

2
'I dream about her in my attic bed' ('Warming Her Pearls')

3
'I'd melt' ('I Wouldn't Thank You for a Valentine')

4
'What will survive of us is love' ('An Arundel Tomb')

5
'Pillow'd upon my fair love's ripening breast' ('Bright Star')

6
'Ah Sweet – The moment eternal –' ('Now')

'Alas! at every breeze I weep –' ('A Song')

'Alas' is a very old English word to express grief or sadness. The verb 'to weep' suggests unhappiness in love too. 'Breeze' suggests stormy weather. This could be an example of a **pathetic fallacy** and be suggestive of threat to the relationship. I think the best fit here is *lost love*.

We need to look closely at the language of a poem to work out the thoughts and feelings that are being expressed by the poet. Despite the **connotations** of the words 'love' and 'relationships' being positive, there are lots of contrasting ways in which the experience is represented in the poems.

Look at the following extracts from poems in the 'Love and relationships' cluster. How does each poem express ideas about love and relationships? Some words and phrases in the first one have been highlighted and annotated.

1

Love is like the wild rose-briar,

Friendship like the holly-tree

The holly is dark when the rose-briar blooms

But which will bloom most constantly?

('Love and Friendship')

Suggests untamed nature, beautiful but dangerous. Idea of love being something threatening.

Doesn't bloom like the rose-briar, but holly is an evergreen plant so will never wilt and die like the rose.

'Constantly' reminds us of 'constancy'—the quality of being faithful and unchanging, perhaps the quality of love most valued in the poem.

Activity 4

1. Make your own highlights and annotations for the three extracts below. Remember, you are trying to think closely about the language of the poem in order to explore the attitudes and feelings towards love and relationships that the poem explores.

2. Can you match each extract to one of the love types talked about earlier? Or perhaps you might come up with a new category.

2

You did not come,

And marching Time drew on, and wore me numb.

('A Broken Appointment')

3

Give back your heart

to itself, to the stranger who has loved you

all your life, whom you ignored

for another, who knows you by heart.

('Love After Love')

4

And I lie here awake,

knowing the pearls are cooling even now

in the room where my mistress sleeps. All night

I feel their absence and I burn.

('Warming Her Pearls')

Activity 5

1. Can you find another poem from the cluster that explores the same theme as one of the poems you have been thinking about?

   Use a table like the one below to think of links between the poems:

Title of each poem in the cluster	Another poem or poems from cluster	Theme shared
'An Arundel Tomb'	'Long Distance II'	Life after love
'In Paris With You'	'I Wouldn't Thank You for a Valentine'	Love explored through humour

2. Compare your choice poems with those of other students. Ask them to explain why they have chosen those poems.

3. Write a paragraph of your own that explores why you have chosen the poem you have. An example could be 'An Arundel Tomb' with the theme of surviving beyond death, so your paragraph could begin something like this:

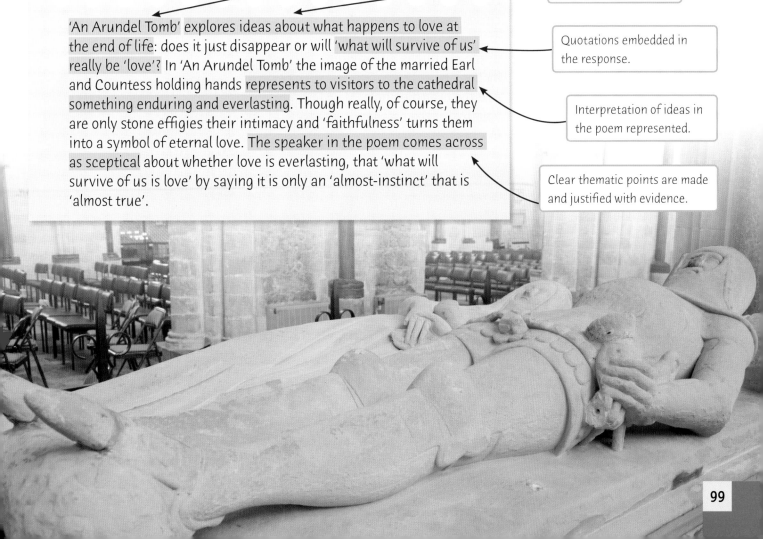

'An Arundel Tomb' explores ideas about what happens to love at the end of life: does it just disappear or will 'what will survive of us' really be 'love'? In 'An Arundel Tomb' the image of the married Earl and Countess holding hands represents to visitors to the cathedral something enduring and everlasting. Though really, of course, they are only stone effigies their intimacy and 'faithfulness' turns them into a symbol of eternal love. The speaker in the poem comes across as sceptical about whether love is everlasting, that 'what will survive of us is love' by saying it is only an 'almost-instinct' that is 'almost true'.

The choice of poem is introduced at the start of the response.

Themes clearly stated.

Quotations embedded in the response.

Interpretation of ideas in the poem represented.

Clear thematic points are made and justified with evidence.

Unit 3 Understanding the theme: Conflict

Learning objectives

- To explore the theme of each of the three clusters and possible meanings or ideas that might be connected

- To focus on the skills of identifying the key themes of the poems in the cluster and to make links to other poems

Thinking about the theme of your cluster

How can we begin to think about the themes and ideas contained in the poems in your cluster? Each of these themes represents something pretty large in human experience, so it figures *we already know* quite a lot about the theme. Perhaps what will be interesting when we study the poems is how what we already know will be reflected, or challenged, by the poems studied?

Activity 1

1. What is 'conflict'? Come up with a one-sentence working definition of the word.

2. Jot down some examples of conflict that you have experienced, for example, conflicts with friends, family members or people in authority. Or you could think about conflict in a more abstract way, such as the *internal conflicts* you have experienced. Share your ideas with a partner.

3. Think about some of the conflicts that you have heard about in the media, anything from small-scale conflicts between individuals, for example, two celebrities in a 'Twitterstorm', to conflicts between large groups or countries. Add these examples to the list you made earlier.

4. Look at the diagram to the right. The circles represent different categories of conflict. The type and scale of the conflict is represented by the size of the circle. Add the examples from your list to the category in which they best fit.

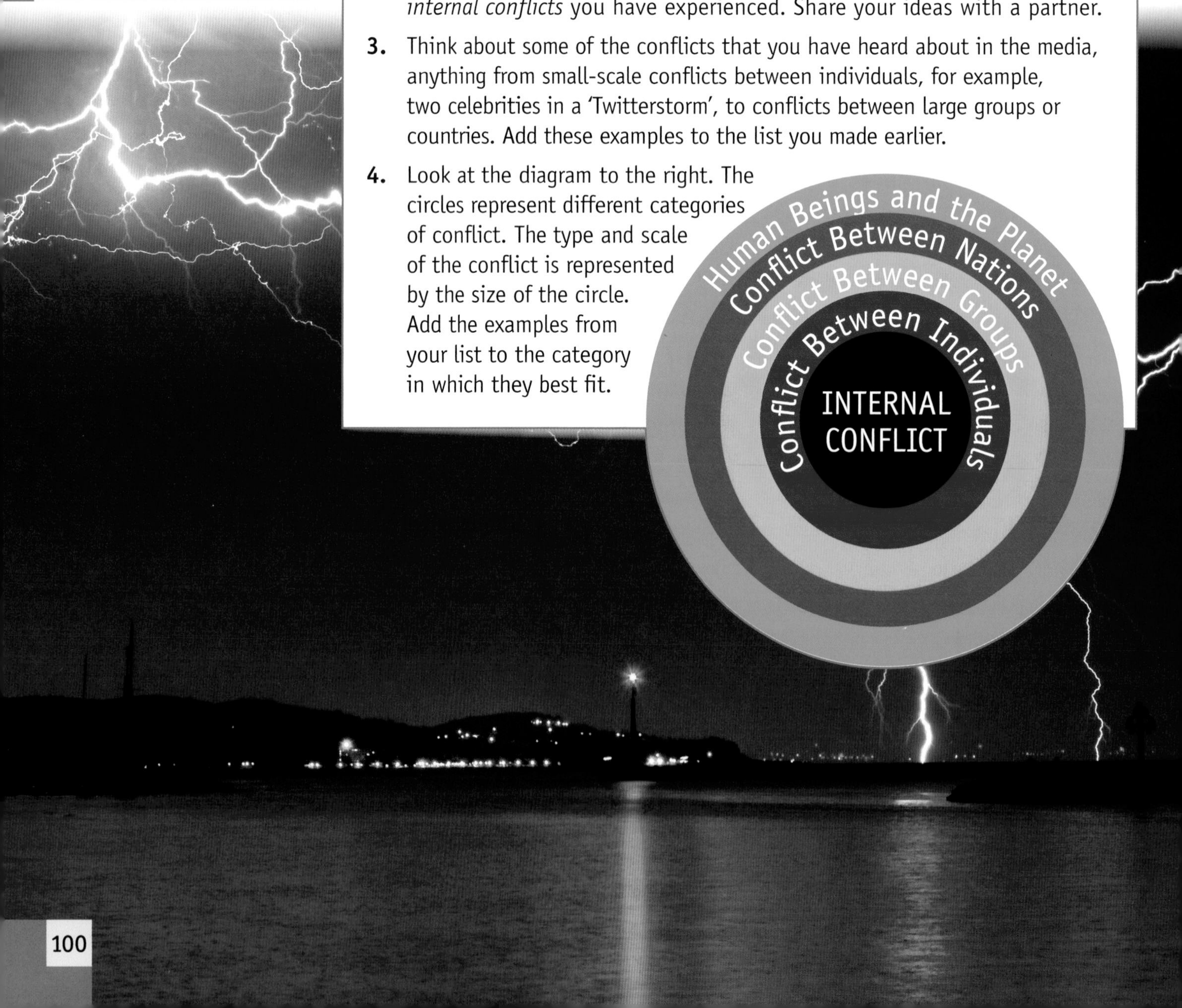

Human Beings and the Planet
Conflict Between Nations
Conflict Between Groups
Conflict Between Individuals
INTERNAL CONFLICT

In the exam, you will be given one poem from the cluster and asked to compare it with another of your choice that has some connections with it. The question might ask you, for example, to think about two poems from the cluster that deal with experiences of war.

When thinking about the themes and ideas in a poem a good starting point is to consider what is suggested by the title.

Here are some of the titles of poems in the 'Conflict' cluster.

'Envy'

'Boat Stealing'

'The Destruction of Sennacherib'

'The Man He Killed'

'Anthem for Doomed Youth'

'Honour Killing'

'Honour' suggests something noble and something morally right. 'Killing' suggests causing death deliberately. How can killing somebody be 'honourable? 'Honour' and 'Killing' feels like an **oxymoron**.

Activity 2

1. Select a title from above. What is suggested by the title alone? Think about definitions of the words, any associations that they have for you, and what kind of conflict is implied by the title.

   For example, look above at a student's ideas about the poem 'Honour Killing'.

2. Try doing the same for the other titles. When you read the poem itself, do the associations of the title match the ideas in the poem?

Poems work by saying the maximum amount in the minimum number of words. Every word counts in a poem so, to explore the themes and ideas in the poetry we are studying, we must look very closely at the language used.

As we will see, the idea of 'conflict' means many different things to the poets in this selection.

Activity 3

Look at the five extracts below from poems in the cluster. By looking closely at particular words and phrases, what can we say about the ideas on conflict that are presented? In the first extract, some words and phrases have been highlighted and annotated as an example.

The use of the first-person pronoun 'I' suggests this is a *conflict between two individuals.*

First the conflict is between the speaker and a 'friend' and then a 'foe'.

By telling his friend about his anger – or wrath – it makes it go away.

1

I was angry with my friend:

I told my wrath, my wrath did end.

I was angry with my foe:

I told it not, my wrath did grow.

('A Poison Tree')

'Foe' is a very old English word for *enemy.* This seems quite a *formal* word, as if the enmity between these two can never change?

Telling his enemy about his anger is unlikely to make their relationship better, but by not telling him the anger has grown and festered. Perhaps the message here is that conflicts are better expressed than bottled up?

2

...and my little boat moved on

Just like a man who walks with stately step

Though bent on speed. It was an act of stealth

And troubled pleasure.

('Boat Stealing')

3

I shot him dead because –

Because he was my foe,

Just so: my foe of course he was;

That's clear enough;

('The Man He Killed')

4

When bombs smashed those mirrors

there was time only to scream.

('What Were They Like?')

5

For the green turtle with her pulsing burden,

in search of the breeding ground.

For her eggs laid in a nest of sickness.

('Lament')

Activity 4

Can you match each extract to one of the conflict types in the circles you looked at on page 100? Or do some fit under a different category of conflict?

Activity 5

1. Can you find another poem from the cluster that explores the same theme as one of the poems you have been thinking about?

    Use a table like the one below to think of links between the poems:

Title of each poem in the cluster	Another poem or poems from cluster	Theme shared
'The Man He Killed'	'Vergissmeinnicht'	Reflections on death of enemy
'Anthem for Doomed Youth'	'What Were They Like?'	Both poems strongly anti-war

2. Compare your choice of poems with those of other students. Ask them to explain why they have chosen those poems.

3. Write a paragraph that explores why you have chosen the poem you have. An example could be 'Vergissmeinnicht', which explores the feelings of death of an individual in enemy combat. Your paragraph could begin something like this:

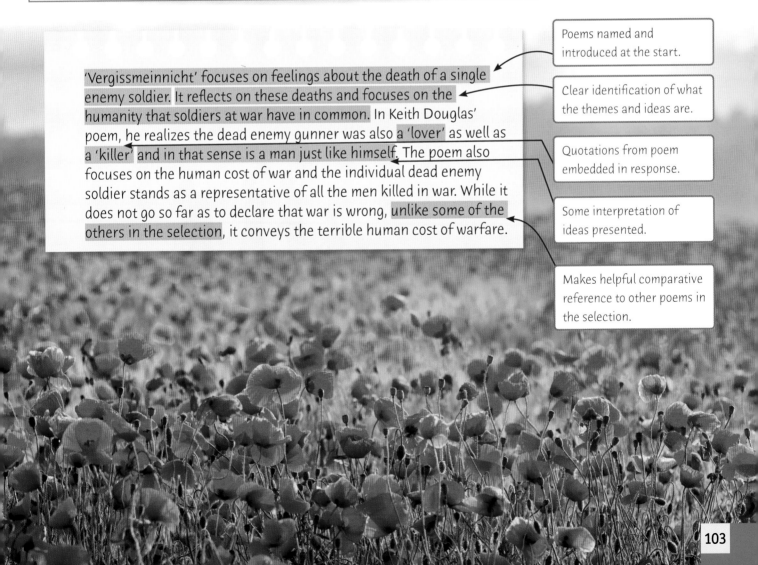

'Vergissmeinnicht' focuses on feelings about the death of a single enemy soldier. It reflects on these deaths and focuses on the humanity that soldiers at war have in common. In Keith Douglas' poem, he realizes the dead enemy gunner was also a 'lover' as well as a 'killer' and in that sense is a man just like himself. The poem also focuses on the human cost of war and the individual dead enemy soldier stands as a representative of all the men killed in war. While it does not go so far as to declare that war is wrong, unlike some of the others in the selection, it conveys the terrible human cost of warfare.

Poems named and introduced at the start.

Clear identification of what the themes and ideas are.

Quotations from poem embedded in response.

Some interpretation of ideas presented.

Makes helpful comparative reference to other poems in the selection.

Unit 4 Understanding the theme: Youth and age

Learning objectives

- To explore the theme of each of the three clusters and possible meanings or ideas that might be connected

- To focus on the skills of identifying the key themes of the poems in the cluster and to make links to other poems

Thinking about the theme of your cluster

How can we begin to think about the themes and ideas contained in the poems in your cluster? Each of these themes represents something pretty large in human experience, so it figures *we already know* quite a lot about the theme. Perhaps what will be interesting when we study the poems is how what we already know will be reflected, or challenged, by the poems studied?

The topic 'Youth and age' suggests two different states: being young and being old. But many of the poems in this cluster represent reflections on the *journey* we all make from one stage to the other, rather than depicting just the one state.

Activity 1

1. What comes to mind when you think of the terms 'youth' and 'age'? Jot down words and associations you have with each term.

   For 'youth', for example, you might have a **synonym** like 'childhood' or 'innocence' and for 'age' you might jot down 'experience'. But you could also consider less obviously connected abstract nouns that can be associated with your word too, like 'freedom' or 'power'.

Key term

Synonym a word or phrase that has the same meaning as another word or phrase

So we have two words that describe two different stages of life. But is there a clear distinction between the two? Is there a specific moment/age when someone stops being 'young' and becomes 'old'? We have all known young people who seem quite 'old' and older people who can seem quite 'young'.

Below is a continuum representing a human life, from young to old. A continuum is a sequence in which each element is quite similar to the ones next to it, but the extremes are distinct.

YOUNG _____ **OLD**

Activity 2

What are some of the key events that mark the journey from youth to age?

1. Draw your own continuum and mark on it what you think the most significant events in this journey are. For example, most people remember starting school.

2. Is there a point on the continuum which best represents the moment when 'youth' gives way to 'age'? Leaving school? Having a child of your own?

The real theme here is the process of *growing up*. In our culture, we tend to regard the process as a positive thing: we praise children for behaving in a 'grown-up' way, and when adults behave in an immature way we tell them they should 'grow up'! It is almost as if childhood is an undesirable state which we should hurry to leave behind.

So it is ironic that, after all that haste to grow up, so much adult time is spent looking back to that relatively brief period in a lifetime that we spend as children. Writers are some of the worst offenders here, with many novels, plays and poems looking back to childhood to seek an understanding of who we are. Many of the poems in this cluster are adult reflections on childhood.

Here are some of the titles of poems in the 'Youth and age' cluster.

> **Tip**
>
> Remember that, when thinking about the themes and ideas in a poem, a good starting point is to consider what is suggested by the title.

'When I have fears that I may cease to be'

'Farther'

'Baby Song'

'Cold Knap Lake'

'My First Weeks'

'Spring and Fall: to a Young Child'

> - The title suggests a record of some kind of early life.
> - It seems a happy and celebratory thing – like something produced by a proud parent.
> - Slightly odd that it is 'My' first weeks rather than 'his' or 'her' or the child's name. Impossible to know what your own first weeks were like.

Activity 3

1. What is suggested by the title alone? Think about definitions for the words and associations that the words have for you, as well as thinking about what kind of youth or age is implied by the title.
   For example, look at one student's thoughts on 'My First Weeks'.

2. Try doing the same for the other titles. When you read the poem itself, do the associations of the title match the ideas in the poem?

Activity 4

Look at the following extracts from poems in the cluster. By looking closely at particular words and phrases, what can we say about the ideas on youth and age that are presented? In the first extract, some words and phrases have been highlighted and annotated. Try doing something similar for the other examples.

> He is, of course, talking hypothetically about being dead.

> Poem begins with what seems like quite a morbid reflection on the poet's own death.

> He doesn't express this in a fearful way though – it all seems quite measured.

1

When I have fears that I may cease to be
Before my pen has glean'd my teeming brain,
Before high pilgraved books, in charact'ry
('When I have fears that I may cease to be')

> But it is based on certainties: he will at some point die and he won't have achieved everything he could have in his life.

> The fact that we know John Keats did die when he was 26 years old makes this opening especially powerful.

2

O, that lone flower recalled to me
My happy childhood's hours
When bluebells seemed like fairy gifts
A prize among the flowers,
('The Bluebell')

3

What past can be yours, O journeying boy
Towards a world unknown,
Who calmly, as if incurious quite
On all at stake, can undertake
This plunge alone?
('Midnight on the Great Western')

4

From the private ease of Mother's womb
I fall into the lighted room.

Why don't they simply put me back,
Where it is warm and wet and black?
('Baby Song')

5

Was I there?
Or is that troubled surface something else
shadowy under the dipped fingers of willows
where satiny mud blooms in cloudiness
after the treading, heavy webs of swans
('Cold Knap Lake')

Activity 5

1. Can you find another poem from the cluster that explores the same theme as one of the poems you have been thinking about?

   Use a table like the one below to think of links between the poems:

Title of each poem in the cluster	Another poem or poems from cluster	Theme shared
'The Bluebell'	'Cold Knap Lake'	Memories of childhood
'Love'	'Farther'	Parents and children

2. Compare your choice of poems with those of other students. Ask them to explain why they have chosen those poems.

3. Write a paragraph that explores why you have selected a poem from the cluster. An example could be 'Cold knap Lake' with childhood memories and feelings as the theme. Your paragraph could begin something like this:

Tip

Remember a poem from the Anthology will firstly be compared with an unseen poem in the exam. You will then be asked to explore a theme with another poem from the Anthology.

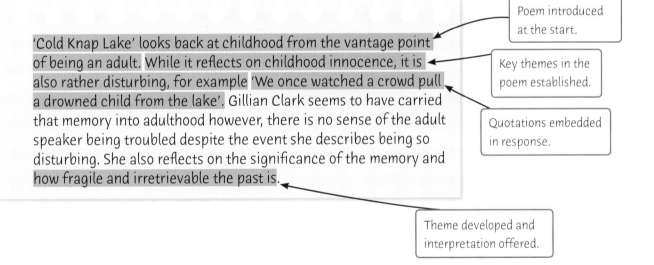

'Cold Knap Lake' looks back at childhood from the vantage point of being an adult. While it reflects on childhood innocence, it is also rather disturbing, for example 'We once watched a crowd pull a drowned child from the lake'. Gillian Clark seems to have carried that memory into adulthood however, there is no sense of the adult speaker being troubled despite the event she describes being so disturbing. She also reflects on the significance of the memory and how fragile and irretrievable the past is.

Poem introduced at the start.

Key themes in the poem established.

Quotations embedded in response.

Theme developed and interpretation offered.

Unit 5 Exploring form and structure

Learning objectives

- To explore form and structure and how poets use both to create meaning and effect

- To learn how to write about form and structure

Exam link

AO2 asks you to: analyse the language, form and structure used by a writer to create meanings and effects.

How does a poem present themes and ideas?

So far, we have been thinking about how the poems in the anthology are grouped into clusters around the broad themes of love and relationships, conflict, and youth and age. It is obviously very important to think about what a poem is saying but lots of different texts, like stories or media texts, present us with themes and ideas. What is special about how a poem does it?

Form and structure

In your exam, you will need to comment on how the poet has used form and structure to create meaning and effects.

Meaning relates to what ideas the poet is presenting us with, such as the doubts and uncertainties of love, or the misery of war, or bitter-sweet memories of a lost childhood. *Effects* are the methods that the poet uses to communicate this meaning to the reader or listener.

But what are you being asked to do when you are asked to analyse *form* and *structure* in poetry? Let's start with some brief definitions.

Form relates to what the poem *is*, what type of poem it is and how it appears on the page. There are many different forms or types of poems; some of the most common appear below.

Ballad: A popular storytelling type of poem recounting heroic, tragic or comic events, often written in four-line stanzas or quatrains.

Dramatic monologue: A poem in which a speaker addresses a silent listener.

Elegy: A sad poem that laments the death of a public person or someone of importance to the poet.

Ode: A formal poem that celebrates a person, object or idea.

Lyric poem: A form of poetry that expresses personal emotions, typically written in the first person. Usually has a regular rhyme scheme and meter.

Sonnet: A 14-line poem, often on the topic of love, and in the case of those written by Shakespeare divided into three quatrains and a rhyming couplet.

When you are writing about form you will need to be able to comment on the features that contribute to that form. Some features are: stanzas, rhyme, lines, syllables, repetition, rhyme, scheme, meter.

Activity 1

Find out what each of the above features is and write an appropriate definition.

Structure relates to the internal organization of the poem, the relationship between different parts of the poem and how it moves towards some kind of conclusion. When you are writing about structure you will need to think about lots of different aspects including:

- the mood and focus of the poem and how it changes

- repeated or echoed ideas and how ideas are built up

- how the lines are written: in stanzas or couplets? All the same length or varied?

- punctuation and pauses in lines (**caesura**).

Form and structure are closely related and the form of a poem will lead to certain structural features. One of the best ways of thinking about the two terms is that when you are talking about form you can describe structural features, and when talking about structure consider the impact of these organizational choices on what the poem is saying.

Analysing form

In the exam, you will be comparing a poem from the anthology cluster you have been studying with an unseen poem.

Read the poem below. It is called 'Remember' and was written in 1849 when the poet, Christina Rossetti, was only 19 years old.

Source text A

'Remember' by Christina Rossetti

Remember me when I am gone away,
      Gone far away into the silent land;
      When you can no more hold me by the hand,
Nor I half turn to go yet turning stay.
Remember me when no more day by day
      You tell me of our future that you plann'd:
      Only remember me; you understand
It will be late to counsel then or pray.
Yet if you should forget me for a while
      And afterwards remember, do not grieve:
      For if the darkness and corruption leave
      A vestige of the thoughts that once I had,
Better by far you should forget and smile
      Than that you should remember and be sad.

Key term

Iambic pentameter the five-beat line made up of unstressed and stressed syllables which Shakespeare uses most frequently in his plays; when unrhymed, this is called blank verse

You might have decided that the poem 'Remember' didn't really fit the definition of a ballad as it does not tell a tragic or comic story, but it does have some qualities of the dramatic monologue, with the speaker directly addressing a silent listener. It's not an elegy because no one has actually died, and it is not really addressing an object or idea, so cannot be called an ode. So sonnet is the best fit, and the fact that it has 14 lines seems to confirm that.

But aren't sonnets usually love poems? A poem imagining the reaction of someone to the speaker's death doesn't *seem* much like a love poem. So you could say that the sonnet breaks that usual tradition of being a love poem.

Alternatively, you could say that because the speaker hasn't *actually* died and the poem does seem to contain behaviours typical of those in love (holding hands, planning a future together, finding it difficult to part), thinking about the sad time after one of them has died serves to make the feelings of love all the *more* intense in the present. So perhaps it does work as a love poem.

Either point of view would be interesting: studying poetry is about exploring possibilities of meaning. There really aren't right and wrong answers.

So 'Remember' is a sonnet. What else could you say about the form of the poem?

- It is a 'Petrarchan' or Italian sonnet, named after the 14th-century Italian poet Francesco Petrarch. This form was imitated by other poets for many centuries.

- The Petrarchan sonnet is divided into two parts: an eight-line section (the octave) followed by a six-line section (the sestet).

- The octave of this kind of sonnet has a regular *abbaabba* rhyme scheme.

- The sestet has one of several rhyme schemes, in this case *cdcece*.

- The poem is written in **iambic pentameter**.

Analysing structure

Tip

Thinking about the structure of a poem can help you to explore the meaning, and build an argument in the exam.

Activity 3

1. Look back at 'Remember' on page 109. Note down the ideas and attitudes that are presented in the octave compared to those that are presented in the sestet. What are the differences between the two parts of the poem? Why has the poet structured her ideas in this way?

2. Write a paragraph to summarize your thoughts and ideas.

Here is an example of how you might comment on the structure in this poem and the effects it may have.

The mood of the poem seems to change after the eighth line. In the first part, the tone seems quite harsh; her departure prior to his is presented as inevitable and he is being instructed to keep her firmly in his memory long after she has gone 'into the silent land'. The tone suggests that she fears he won't remember her and needs to be reminded.

But in the last six lines the tone lightens, it becomes more accepting and forgiving of him if he should 'forget me for a while'. She doesn't want him to be 'sad' after she has died.

So the structure of the poem with its division of octave and sestet reflects the shift in tone and attitude in the poem.

Activity 4

1. Write a paragraph to say how Christina Rossetti's choices of form and structure in this poem help to present her ideas and feelings.

2. Now choose a poem from your anthology cluster. What can you say about form and structure and how this creates meaning in the poem? Jot down your ideas in a table like the one below.

Title of the poem	Form	Structure	Effects created
'Bright Star' by John Keats	'Shakespearian' sonnet, three quatrains followed by a rhyming couplet.	Argument divided into two sections, like an Italian sonnet.	Presents one idea (the steadfast star) and then modifies it (faithfulness in relationships).
'Flag' by John Agard	Regular form of five three-line stanzas; these resemble stripes on a national flag. It ends with a rhyming couplet.	Structured as a conversation between someone innocent (a child?) and someone experienced.	Creates the effect of the two speakers on a journey of discovery that builds to the implications of flag-following at the end.
'Cold Knap Lake' by Gillian Clarke	Two stanzas of four lines, followed by six lines, ending with a rhyming couplet.	The four-line stanzas describe the event, and the six-line ones reflect further on it before the 'conclusion' of the couplet.	Creates the sense of this event being a blend of what is remembered and what is imagined.

Read the following poem. It is called 'Piano' and was written in 1918 by D. H. Lawrence.

Source text B

'Piano' by D. H. Lawrence

Softly, in the dusk, a woman is singing to me;
Taking me back down the vista of years, till I see
A child sitting under the piano, in the boom of the tingling strings
And pressing the small, poised feet of a mother who smiles as she sings.

In spite of myself, the insidious mastery of song
Betrays me back, till the heart of me weeps to belong
To the old Sunday evenings at home, with winter outside
And hymns in the cosy parlour, the tinkling piano our guide.

So now it is vain for the singer to burst into clamour
With the great black piano appassionato. The glamour
Of childish days is upon me, my manhood is cast
Down in the flood of remembrance, I weep like a child for the past.

Activity 5

1. What can you say about the form and structure of this poem?

2. How do the form and structure of the poem relate to what the poet is saying in the poem?

   Share some ideas about both of these questions with a partner.

Putting your skills into practice

When writing about an unseen poem in the exam, the question will ask you to relate the theme of the poem to one of the poems you have studied in your cluster of the anthology, for example:

a. Compare how the speakers in these poems express feelings towards past events.

You should consider:

- Ideas and attitudes in each poem
- Tone and atmosphere in each poem
- The effects of the language and structure used

Activity 6

1. Read D. H. Lawrence's poem 'Piano' on page 112 and imagine that it is the unseen poem in your exam. Write part of an exam answer that focuses on the effects created by the form and structure of the poem.

2. Choose another poem from your anthology cluster that also focuses on past events. Compare some of the ideas about the form and structure of that poem with 'Piano'.

3. Below is an example of how a student has written about the form and structure of 'Piano'. Read the examiner's comments and identify ways you can improve your answers to questions 1 and 2.

Whole paragraph relates to the first of the three stanzas in the poem.

Identifies the form of the poem.

Describes the structure of the poem and the rhyme scheme.

Interpretations offered, but using the word 'seems' suggests there are alternative viewpoints.

Thinks about this poem as a 'lyric' and also picks up on the music theme in the title.

Awareness of the significant change of tone in the second stanza.

Explains how the structure relates to the development of the ideas in the poem.

Precise and detailed comment.

Arrives at an interpretation at the end of the paragraph.

Effective variety in sentence types.

Continues focus on the structure of the poem as it moves backwards and forward in time.

Analysis ends with an overall interpretation of the poem.

'Piano' is a simple lyric poem of three stanzas with a regular repeated *aabb* rhyme scheme. The three stanzas develop the situation: a man is listening to the singing of a woman and hearing this transports him back in memory to his childhood. The first stanza seems to present this as a happy or nostalgic memory. The music takes him 'back down the vista of years' as if he is powerless to stop this happening. He arrives at a scene where 'a child' is under a piano which 'a mother' is playing. The use of the indefinite article in 'a child' and 'a mother' is surprising because we assume the child is him and the mother *his* mother.

It is music that has transported him into memory, and just as a piece of music is divided into different sections with different ideas and tones so too is this poem in the division of the stanzas. In the second stanza, he is fully immersed in the memory of childhood but the happy tone seems to have changed. He has been taken back into this memory 'in spite of himself'. The memory is certainly a happy one: 'Sunday evenings at home, with winter outside' and the 'cosy parlour' but the speaker 'weeps to belong'. We realize in this stanza that to remember these times is painful because they can be recalled but cannot be reclaimed.

The third stanza returns to the present of the opening line of the poem. The speaker's mood has become progressively worse. Not only is he saddened by not being able to reclaim past events, but also it has affected his appreciation of the present. The singer sings in vain. He becomes vulnerable, lost and childlike at the end of the poem weeping like a child. It is as if he belongs in neither place.

Unit 6 Analysing language

Looking at language in a poem

To respond to a poem is to respond to the language in which it is written. Interesting poems present a situation for the reader through *what* the poet says, and also through *how* the poet says it. As we read and listen to that language, meanings in the poem will start to appear.

Some poetry can have a reputation for being 'difficult', for using a special **register** of 'poetic' language that only certain people can understand. Some poetry *is* difficult, perhaps because it is presenting complex emotions and ideas or because it was written in a language that feels quite different to contemporary English. Because of this, some people can feel daunted by poetry. The poet Adrian Mitchell said 'most people ignore most poetry because most poetry ignores most people'.

Not all poetry is so challenging. Much poetry is written in a language that is quite familiar to us, and even those poems that use more difficult language can become understandable as we think carefully about the words and phrases used. The more we think about the language of a poem, the more will be revealed.

Language and context

It is important to remember that poetry is the one area of your exam where you are not assessed on your understanding of *context*. However, knowing something about the context in which a poem was written can help you to explore the poem's meaning and the language used.

- Who wrote the poem?

- When was it written?

- What were the circumstances in which the poem was written?

This is particularly the case when the poem was written some time ago or in a different culture.

Activity 1

Knowing details about the context in which the poems in your anthology cluster were written can be really helpful to your understanding of language. Find out about who wrote the poem, when it was written and what circumstances it was written in. You could create a table like the one below.

Cluster	Poem	The poet
Love and relationships	'A Broken Appointment' (1887)	Thomas Hardy
Conflict	'Anthem for Doomed Youth' (1917)	Wilfred Owen
Youth and age	'Out, Out–' (1916)	Robert Frost

The language of titles

The language of the title of a poem is also worth exploring. How can you describe the language of a poem title in your cluster? Is it a literal title that refers to a place or event, like 'Cold Knap Lake' or 'Boat Stealing'? Or is it an allegorical title like 'A Poison Tree', a childlike title such as 'My First Weeks', a punning title like 'Farther' or a confessional title like 'When I have fears that I may cease to be'?

Activity 2

Make a list of the titles and try describing the language of each and the impact of that title on the reader. You could use a table like the one below.

Title	Type of language	Impact on the reader of this language choice
'Dusting the Phone'	Domestic, everyday, unremarkable language	The mundane title creates impact when you realize it is a heartfelt love poem.
'The Bluebell'	The language of nature	Associations of joy and optimism with this spring flower, yet the poem is about mourning a lost childhood.

Tip

Remember, when talking about 'meaning' in a poem it is not a single or fixed thing. What a poem means can change over time, and as a result of the life experiences of the person reading it.

The language of the speaker's voice

To explore the language of a poem is to explore the 'voice' in which it is written. A good starting point is to think about the viewpoint from which the events in the poem are being presented to us.

Is the poem written from a first-person point of view, where the speaker uses the pronoun 'I'? Or in the second person, referring to 'you'? Or in the third person, where the poet uses 'she', 'he' or 'they'?

Different forms and styles of poem suit different perspectives. Poems that seem confessional, intimate and autobiographical tend to be in the first person. When the second person is used, the experience is made to seem universal rather than individual and the reader is drawn into the events. And when the poet wants to create the sense that events are being reported on they might use the third person.

Activity 3

1. For each of the poems in your anthology cluster, decide which point of view has been used.

2. Why do you think the poet has chosen to write from this perspective?

Denotation and connotation in language

Denotation refers to a word's literal or dictionary definition and *connotation* refers to all the associations a person might make, positive and negative, with that word. Words carry both denotative and connotative meanings. In order to present ideas that are vivid and original, poets often use language that has strong connotative associations.

Key term

Imagery the use of descriptive or figurative language to help a reader visualize an idea.

The associations we make with the words in poetry will determine how successfully the poem works for us. The connotative power of words creates the **imagery** that sparks our sensual response to the poem: what we can imagine seeing, hearing, smelling, touching and tasting in the world of the poem.

Below is another poem by Langston Hughes entitled 'Dreams'.

1 'Hold fast' **2** 'dreams' **3** 'broken-winged bird' **4** 'fly' **5** 'a barren field'

Activity 4

Consider the above words and phrases from the poem:

1. Jot down the denotative or literal meaning of each word or phrase.

2. Add any connotative meanings that the word or phrase has for you.

3. The 'meaning' of the poem lies in these connotative meanings. What do you think the poet is saying?

Source text A

'Dreams' by Langston Hughes

Hold fast to dreams
For if dreams die
Life is a broken-winged bird
That cannot fly.

Hold fast to dreams
For when dreams go
Life is a barren field
Frozen with snow.

The language of sound

When you read poems, both the ones in your anthology and unseen ones, it is important to remember that poetry is a spoken medium: poems are designed to be recited and listened to. In order for poems to work in this way, poets need to include in the language all kinds of sound effects so that the poem comes alive for us when we hear it. You have already thought how the particular sounds of a spoken voice tell us things about the character of the speaker. But there are lots of other sound effects that can be created in the language of a poem.

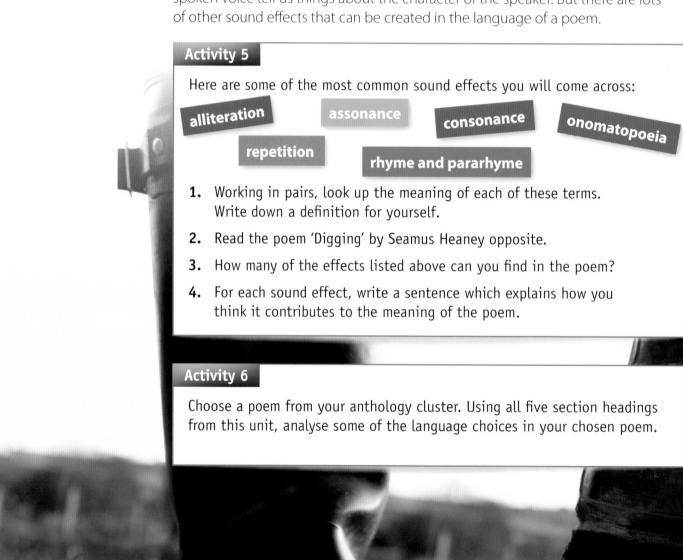

Activity 5

Here are some of the most common sound effects you will come across:

alliteration   assonance   consonance   onomatopoeia

repetition   rhyme and pararhyme

1. Working in pairs, look up the meaning of each of these terms. Write down a definition for yourself.

2. Read the poem 'Digging' by Seamus Heaney opposite.

3. How many of the effects listed above can you find in the poem?

4. For each sound effect, write a sentence which explains how you think it contributes to the meaning of the poem.

Activity 6

Choose a poem from your anthology cluster. Using all five section headings from this unit, analyse some of the language choices in your chosen poem.

Source text B

'Digging' by Seamus Heaney

Between my finger and my thumb
The squat pen rests; snug as a gun.

Under my window, a clean rasping sound
When the spade sinks into gravelly ground:
My father, digging. I look down

Till his straining rump among the flowerbeds
Bends low, comes up twenty years away
Stooping in rhythm through potato drills
Where he was digging.

The coarse boot nestled on the lug, the shaft
Against the inside knee awas levered firmly.
He rooted out tall tops, buried the bright edge deep
To scatter new potatoes that we picked,
Loving their cool hardness in our hands.

By God, the old man could handle a spade.
Just like his old man.

My grandfather cut more turf in a day
Than any other man on Toner's bog.
Once I carried him milk in a bottle
Corked sloppily with paper. He straightened up
To drink it, then fell to right away
Nicking and slicing neatly, heaving sods
Over his shoulder, going down and down
For the good turf. Digging.

The cold smell of potato mould, the squelch and slap
Of soggy peat, the curt cuts of an edge
Through living roots awaken in my head.
But I've no spade to follow men like them.

Between my finger and my thumb
The squat pen rests.
I'll dig with it.

Unit 7 Making comparisons

Learning objectives

- To compare two poems in the exam
- To identify ways to make links, for example, thematic links, stylistic links
- To write an answer comparing two extracts

What will you need to do in the exam?

Section A of the GCSE English Literature Paper 2 exam has two parts.

In part a., one poem from your anthology cluster and one unseen poem will be printed on the exam paper. You will be asked a question that makes links between the two poems and the theme of the cluster.

You will also be given three bullet points to remind you to consider:

- ideas and attitudes in each poem
- tone and atmosphere in each poem
- the effects of the language and structure used.

These points relate to the requirement in AO2: analyse the language, form and structure used by a writer to create meanings and effects. It is also expected that you will be able to do the following:

☑ Maintain a critical style – not too chatty, keep your writing reasonably formal

☑ Use subject terminology – be able to apply the terms used in the glossary

☑ Use textual references – use short, relevant quotations in your answer

☑ Develop an informed personal response – engage with the poems and suggest different interpretations

☑ Make connections between the poems – explore how the poems relate to one another

☑ Show some understanding of the context in which the poem was written – how might the circumstances in which the poem was written be relevant to the question?

☑ Use a range of vocabulary and sentence types – create some variety in your writing.

So in part a., you will be comparing one poem you know with one you don't. You will be thinking about the relationship between the two poems and focusing on how the unseen poem compares in its presentation of ideas with the poem you have studied.

Thinking about the key words in the question

Look at the three sample questions, one for each of the anthology clusters, on page 121. This is how part a. will be presented in the exam.

Love and relationships

a. Compare how the two poems present love and relationships.

Conflict

a. Compare how the two poems present the impact of conflict on people's lives.

Youth and age

a. Compare how the two poems present memories of the past.

You should consider:

- Ideas and attitudes in each poem
- Tone and atmosphere in each poem
- The effects of the language and structure used

Activity 1

1. Jot down what you think the word 'compare' means.

2. How similar is your definition to this one from the Oxford English Dictionary?

   '**Compare** *verb*: To mark or point out the similarities or differences of (two or more things).'

In the activity above, you probably wrote something about comparison being about looking at the *similarities* between things, but what about *differences*?

When thinking about how to compare poems, it is important to keep this in mind. The unseen poem will, of course, have links with the anthology poem but it won't be *the same*. In fact, the differences between the poems are likely to be more significant than the similarities. All poems explore themes and ideas in different ways. As well as thinking about connections between the two, be prepared to write about the different ways the unseen poem tackles the theme compared to the anthology poem. This might be in terms of the tone, attitude, language choices, or the form and structure.

What you will be doing is discussing an aspect of the theme of your anthology cluster across two poems. The focus will be something very central to both the anthology poem and the unseen poem.

Comparing two poems

So what are the main areas that you are going to focus on in your comparison of the two poems?

- Topic: What is being described in each poem?
- Theme: How does the topic of each poem relate to a broader theme?
- Tone and attitude: How is the attitude of the speaker presented to the reader through the tone of voice?
- Language choices: What are the most significant features of language in the two poems?
- Form and structure: What can you say about the type of poem each is and how they are organized?
- Impact on the reader: How does the poem make you feel as a reader?

This poem on the left leaves a lot of things unstated, so don't worry if parts of it seem a little unclear. As you read it, think about the relationships in the poem, between the 'I' figure and the 'you' figure, and between the 'you' figure and the mother and father. Are there questions that the poem doesn't answer for you?

Source text A

'Homecoming' by Simon Armitage

Think, two things on their own and both at once.
The first, that exercise in trust, where those in front
stand with their arms spread wide and free-fall
backwards, blind, and those behind take all the weight.

The second, one canary-yellow cotton jacket
on a cloakroom floor, uncoupled from its hook,
becoming scuffed and blackened underfoot. Back home
the very model of a model of a mother, yours, puts
two and two together, makes a proper fist of it
and points the finger. Temper, temper. Questions
in the house. You seeing red. Blue murder. Bed.

Then midnight when you slip the latch and sneak
no further than the phonebox at the corner of the street;
I'm waiting by the phone, although it doesn't ring
because it's sixteen years or so before we'll meet.
Retrace that walk towards the garden gate; in silhouette
a father figure waits there, wants to set things straight.

These ribs are pleats or seams. These arms are sleeves.
These fingertips are buttons, or these hands can fold
into a clasp, or else these fingers make a zip
or buckle, you say which. Step backwards into it
and try the same canary-yellow cotton jacket, there
like this, for size again. It still fits.

Activity 2

1. Read the poem out loud or 'aloud in your head'.

2. Make notes on the poem to answer these questions:
   - What does the title of the poem suggest?
   - How many lines and how many stanzas are there?
   - What do you notice about rhyme and rhythm?
   - Are the lines end-stopped or does the poet use **enjambment**?
   - Are there difficult or unclear words and phrases?
   - Who is speaking? Who is being spoken to?
   - What are the main events that the poem describes?
   - What are the main themes that come out of the described event?
   - How is the poem organized or structured?
   - What do you like about the poem? What aspects are you able to relate to?

3. Create a simple table like this. (The blank column will be used in Activity 3.) Looking at your annotations, what points do you want to make under each heading?

	'Homecoming'		Questions about the poems
Topic			
Theme			
Tone and attitude			
Language choices			
Form and structure			
Impact on the reader			

4. In the fourth column, make a note of any questions you have about parts of the poem that might seem less clear.

5. Share your ideas with another pair/group. Did they make similar points? Can you answer any of their questions and vice versa?

Stretch

'Homecoming' is really a poem about trust; what happens when we 'free-fall/backwards, blind, and those behind take all the weight'. Write an account or short story exploring ideas of someone putting their complete trust in another person.

Enjambment a run-on line with no punctuation, which should be read without pausing

Activity 3

1. Look back at the poems in your anthology cluster and choose *one* of them to compare with the unseen poem, 'Homecoming'. It doesn't matter if the poem you choose is quite different in the ideas it presents.

2. Add ideas on this poem to the blank column of your table started in Activity 2.

3. When you have completed your table, use it to help you answer the question on page 121 that relates to your cluster. Think of your answer in *three* sections:

   - Step 1 is your introduction where you make some connections between the two poems and relate this to the title.

   - Step 2 is the main part of the response in which you discuss both poems in detail and make connections between them. You can use a lot of the information you have collected for your table in this section.

   - Step 3 is your conclusion. Here, you can bring in your personal response and discuss how effective you think the poems are in presenting ideas and feelings.

Here are some extracts from student responses, one from each of the three sections, with comments on how effective they are.

Step 1 for the Love and relationships cluster

'Homecoming' by Simon Armitage and 'Long Distance II' by Tony Harrison are both poems that look back at events from the past that have had a lasting impact. Both poems deal with really important relationships in people's lives: with a parent in 'Long Distance II' and, it is implied, with a partner in 'Homecoming'. Though the events, and how they are recalled, are of course different, the idea of the impact of conflict with a parent is central to both. But there are significant differences. 'Long Distance II' is a sad poem, the guilt the son feels about his lack of sympathy for his father can't now be resolved, but in 'Homecoming' there is a sense that things can be 'retraced' and a different outcome achieved.

Both poems and poets named in this introduction. A simple and effective introduction to the comparison.

Clear connection established between poems.

More specific link and connection stated here.

Good to talk about differences as well as similarities.

Interpretation and personal response.

Step 2 for the Conflict cluster

'A Poison Tree' and 'Homecoming' are of course very different poems and around two hundred years separates their writing, but in both the implications in people's lives of unresolved conflict is made clear. William Blake's 'A Poison Tree' shows how anger with someone can feed on itself and grow into something dangerous and destructive that eventually 'kills' his enemy or 'foe'. There is an extended metaphor of plant growth in the poem: his anger is seen as an organic thing that grows and eventually 'bears fruit' and produces an 'apple bright' that tempts and then poisons his enemy. The speaker actively encourages that growth by tending the plant: watering and 'sunning' it. The outcome of this in the final quatrain of the poem is disturbing: not only has this cultivation of the plant killed somebody, but also the speaker is 'glad' about it.

However, in Simon Armitage's 'Homecoming' the conflict that the subject of the poem has experienced as a child is eventually resolved and some of the damaging consequences that we see in Blake's poem of conflict 'growing' poisonously are avoided. The memory of the fight with a mother over a damaged jacket has lingered it seems for sixteen years, but through 'an exercise of trust' and loving support that conflict can be revisited and all its power to grow and 'poison' are destroyed.

> Demonstrates knowledge of context of the anthology poem.

> Embedded quotations from the poems.

> Terminology related to the structure of the poem is used.

> Transitional phrases like 'however', 'on the other hand' and so on are useful in organizing comparative work.

> Links back to previously discussed poem.

Step 3 for the Youth and age cluster

Both Simon Armitage's 'Homecoming' and Gillian Clarke's 'Cold Knap Lake' powerfully evoke memories from the past: a conflict between a mother and child over a damaged coat and an incident where a child is saved from drowning, and then beaten by her father. All of us have memories from the past and these two poems deal with how we cope with these memories in later life and what they continue to mean to us. In both cases the memories are very specific, it's as if memory lies in the details – like the 'canary-yellow jacket' and the 'wartime cotton frock'. And that seems very true to life: memory is sensual, we remember how things looked and sounded and tasted. Because we all revisit and reimagine events from the past, both of these poems deal with familiar processes even though the memories are unique.

> Sense of personal response to the poems.

> Develops personal response, relating events in the poem to real life but avoids doing it in too personal or too individual a way.

Unit 8 Getting ready for the exam

Learning objectives

- To understand the exam questions
- To time and plan a response
- To write a response including an introduction and conclusion and using quotes and textual references

Tip

Use poems from the two clusters that you have not studied to practise responding to unseen poems.

The exam question

In Section A of Paper 2 of your GCSE English Literature exam, all the questions are divided into two parts. In the exam, you will answer *both* parts of the question on the poetry cluster you have studied.

- Part a. will ask you to compare a poem from your cluster with an unseen poem.
- Part b. will ask you to explore another poem of your choice your cluster.

Planning your response

You will be assessed as follows:

Assessment Objective		Part A: Comparing a seen and unseen extract	Part B: Exploring another moment in your set text
A01:	**Critical interpretation** and textual support	40%	50%
A02:	**Language analysis**	60%	50%
A03:	Understanding of **context**	Not assessed	Not assessed

You are advised to spend *1 hour and 15 minutes* on Section A: 45 minutes on part a., the comparison of the unseen poem with the cluster poem, and 30 minutes on the single poem from your cluster in part b. The previous unit in this chapter covered part a., and in this section we will look at how to prepare for writing about your anthology poems in part b.

The part b. question will ask you to select and write about one poem from your cluster that best fits the question you have been asked. The question will be linked to the focus of the part a. question. For example, for the 'Love and relationships' cluster might be:

---

a. Compare how the speakers in these poems express feelings of being *let down in love*.

You should consider:

- Ideas and attitudes in each poem
- Tone and atmosphere in each poem
- The effects of the language and structure used

[20]

AND

b. Explore in detail one other poem from your anthology which expresses *doubt or uncertainty in relationships*.

[20]

For 'Conflict' the focus on *effects of war* in part a. becomes:

> **b.** Explore in detail one other poem from your anthology that presents lives transformed by conflict.

And for 'Youth and age' the *relationship between fathers and sons* in part a. becomes:

> **b.** Explore in detail one other poem from your anthology which presents a relationship between a parent and child.

So in this part of the question you are exploring a poem of your choice from your cluster *in detail* and relating it to the question asked. The question will be broad and for each of these questions there will be a range of poems from the cluster that you could select. But it is obviously important that you choose a poem that relates to the question and one that you are confident in writing about.

How to choose a poem that will work well for the question

As you have just 30 minutes to answer this question, you will need to quickly select a suitable poem and plan your response. So what's the best way to approach this question?

Activity 1

1. Look at the sample part b. questions. Which of the poems in your cluster would fit the question? Look at the table below where one poem has been suggested for each of the questions. Draw a similar table yourself and add the names of other poems that you think would fit in the third column and the reasons for your choice in the fourth column.

Cluster	Question focus	Poem choices	Reasons
Love and relationships	Doubt and uncertainty in relationships	'Warming Her Pearls'	Poem deals with the pain of unrequited love
Conflict	Lives transformed by conflict	'Vergissmeinnicht'	Presents the death of an enemy soldier as human tragedy
Youth and age	Relationship between a parent and a child	'Cold Knap Lake'	Complex emotions of a young girl, her feelings about her mother

Here is one possible approach to a response to the 'Love and relationships' question.

Step 1

Begin by directly addressing the key words in the question (for example, doubt and uncertainty in relationships). Even though you will be writing about a single poem in this question, it is good to introduce discussion of that poem by putting it into a broader context. For example:

> Even though this is a response to a single poem, it can be effective to reference the whole cluster.

> Specific focus of the question related to the cluster as a whole.

> Returning to the words of the question makes the response seem well focused.

Not all the poems in the 'Love and relationships' cluster of the anthology present relationships that are happy and fulfilled. In these poems love is not always requited and more of the poems present a yearning for love between people who are separate from one another, than celebrate togetherness in relationships. Perhaps feelings of doubt and uncertainty in relationships are central to love poetry? In these poems, the experience of love seems to create accompanying feelings of loss, of sorrow, jealousy and anxiety. So doubt and uncertainty are central to the experience of many of the speakers in this selection of poems.

Next, you can introduce the poem you have selected and relate it to the question topic.

> Good to refer to the name of the poet as well as the title the first time it is used in the response. A poem from the anthology.

> Relates specific poem to the topic.

> Describes why the relationship is one characterized by doubt and uncertainty.

> Quotations from the poem embedded in the response.

Carol Ann Duffy's 'Warming Her Pearls' is a love poem that is full of doubt and uncertainty because it describes a relationship that exists only in the imagination of the speaker. The gulf in status between the maid and her mistress means the relationship is never likely to be realized. The doubt and jealousy implied by the speaker being alone in her attic bed picturing her mistress 'dancing with tall men' suggests this is a love that brings as much pain as it does happiness. Significantly the speaker is alone at the start, and at the end, of the poem.

> Overall a clear and effective introduction to task, cluster and poem.

Step 2

Start to explore your chosen poem in detail. Remember that in this section you will want to discuss the *themes and ideas* in the poem, the *tone and attitude* presented, *sound effects* in the poem, the *language choices* made and to consider the *form and structure* of the poem.

Here is an approach to this section of a response to the 'Conflict' question.

> This, too, is an anthology poem.

> Reasons for the choice of this poem for this task clearly explained.

Several of the poems in the 'Conflict' cluster present lives transformed by the conflict of war. Keith Douglas' 'Vergissmeinnicht' presents several lives transformed by conflict: the speaker of the poem, the enemy soldier and his sweetheart and, by implication, all of us on whose behalf men and women go to war. The poem forces us to confront the reality of war and the death of an enemy soldier is presented to us as being one of waste and human tragedy. This is as far removed from poems that celebrate valour and heroism in war as you can get.

The horror of the discovery of the dead soldier creeps up on us in the poem. We don't know at first who the speaker is and what his attitudes might be. The opening line, 'Three weeks gone and the combatants gone' with the repeated 'gone' reads almost as if it is a hastily written factual report. But 'nightmare ground' is highly emotive and the reader suspects this is no casual use of the word 'nightmare' and that the speaker is haunted by previous events in this place. The first description of the 'soldier sprawling in the sun' suggests relaxation rather than death, and the rapid movement between these different tones in the opening stanza is disorientating for the reader. We discover in the second stanza that the enemy soldier had previously shot the speaker's tank with such force it was 'like the entry of a demon'. The diabolical nature of this simile suggests the speaker would have every reason to hate his enemy. But 'Look' says the speaker at the start of the third stanza, the imperative verb demands that we don't turn away from the disturbing juxtaposition of the picture and message from Steffi and the sight of the soldier's decaying body. 'We see him almost with content' says the speaker. 'Content' or contempt? Is he pleased the enemy soldier is dead? But then he describes the sad message from Steffi with such tenderness? And who is 'we'? He and the other soldiers? Or all of us? The attitudes of the speaker are difficult to be sure about, as if the soldier himself can't quite process these events. War is messy and contradictory: definite attitudes are hard to maintain.

What we notice most about the rhyme in this poem is the use of half rhyme. 'Gone' is rhymed with 'sun' which perhaps creates the sense of the life-giving properties of the sun having departed. 'Gun', 'on', 'one', and 'demon' are half-rhymed and, more disturbingly, so are 'spoil' and 'girl', which creates a link to the end of the poem which suggests that something of Steffi has died with her loved-one. The rhyme unsettles the reader just as the events being described do. The alliterative 'soldier sprawling' in the first stanza links to another alliteration of the 'soldier singled' by death in the final stanza.

There is much language variety in Keith Douglas' poem from the use of the matter-of-fact language of reporting, to the metaphors of 'nightmare ground', the personification of 'frowning barrel' and the simile of 'like the entry of a demon', the use of the imperative verb 'Look', and the tender colloquialism of 'his girl', the disturbing 'content' he feels when coming across the body, and the graphic language that describes that body. The use of 'killer' in the final stanza seems unforgiving at the end.

The poem is comprised of six quatrains. The structure is that of a journey in which the reader joins the speaker and his fellow soldiers as they arrive back at their 'nightmare ground', through the inspection of the gun and the discovery of the dead soldier and the picture and message from Steffi. The last two stanzas mark a change in the structure. The change in mood as the poem begins to reflect on the implications of what has been witnessed is marked by the use of the coordinating conjunction 'But' at the start of the fifth stanza and the preposition 'For' at the start of the sixth.

An informed personal response here.

Quotations embedded.

Use of 'the reader' rather than 'I' creates sense of objectivity.

Close analysis of the language of the poem and how this creates the attitude and tone of the poem.

Effective to use simple grammatical labels such as this.

Demonstrates command of terminology.

To speculate on meanings helpfully suggests that the meaning is not fixed.

Broadens out to think of the context in which the poem was written.

As well as spotting the feature – half rhyme – an effect of this feature in the poem is described.

Critical terminology accurately used.

Specific examples used to illustrate the variety of language choices.

Simple statement of the structure of the poem worth making.

Develops ideas about the structure here and how this impacts on how we read the poem.

Structure discussed in relation to particular words and phrases.

Step 3

This section is the conclusion to your answer. It allows you to return to the central focus of the question and to demonstrate what the assessment objectives call an 'informed personal response'. By this, they mean the opportunity for you to reflect on the impact of the poem. For example, you might want to say that the poem is moving, or powerful or humorous and explain why.

Here is an example of a response to the 'Youth and age' question.

> An anthology poem.

> Question topic reintroduced in the conclusion.

> Summarizes the parent–child relationships presented in the poem.

> Reader response to the poem.

> Personal response to the poem presented in terms of 'the reader' rather than individual.

'Cold Knap Lake' by Gillian Clarke presents two parallel parent and child relationships: that of the speaker and her parents and the 'drowned' child with her parent who thrashes her for 'almost drowning'. The speaker presents her parents in positive terms. Her mother is a 'heroine' who gives 'a stranger's child her breath' and her father delivers the poor child back to her home. The cruelty of the child's parent beating her creates a sense of shock for the reader and this act along with her near drowning in the lake suggests that she is a neglected child. The speaker, we assume, has a happy childhood yet even so there as a sense of the speaker's exclusion as the other child is held 'bleating and rosy in my mother's hands'. My mother's hands. 'Was I there?' she asks. The question considers if she *really* saw this happen and also a child's sense of exclusion. Did I matter? This complex set of emotions of a child's feelings towards a parent are powerfully presented in the poem.

> Effective summative sentence to conclude the response.

> Interpretation – but presented as a possibility rather than a fact.

Activity 2

1. Choose a sample question for the cluster you have been studying. The marks that would be available for a part b. question in the exam appear in brackets.

> b. **Love and relationships.** Explore in detail one poem from your anthology that uses humour to present feelings about relationships.
> [20]

> b. **Conflict.** Explore one poem from your anthology that presents feelings of guilt about conflict.
> [20]

> b. **Youth and age.** Explore one poem from your anthology that presents the experience of being a child.
> [20]

2. Think about which of the poems you could use for this question and the reasons why you think it would fit.

3. Using the three-section structure, plan and write an answer to the question. Spend 30 minutes on your writing.

Tip

When writing about poetry, don't assume the speaker and the poet are necessarily the same person. Use the term 'speaker' or 'persona' to describe the voice.

Progress check

Now you have reached the end of the chapter you should be gaining confidence in your understanding of the poems in your anthology cluster, and how to talk about them in the exam. Use the questions below to check your knowledge and understanding.

	I still have some questions about this	I am sure I understand this	I am confident I can give clear explanations
I understand the theme of my anthology cluster.			
I have some understanding of all 15 poems in the cluster.			
I can comment on some aspects of the form and structure of each of the poems.			
I can explore key words and phrases from each poem and say something about them.			
I can use some poetic terminology in my discussion.			
I can find points of similarity and difference between studied and unseen poems.			
I understand how the questions will be structured in my exam.			

4 Shakespeare

Component Overview

- You will prepare one Shakespeare play for one question in Section B of Paper 2: Exploring poetry and Shakespeare.

- One option for this question is extract-based, where the extract should be used as a springboard into a wider discussion of the play.

- The alternative option for this question is a whole-text essay, which should explore two or three moments from the play in close detail, before drawing a clear conclusion.

- There are 40 marks for the Shakespeare question so it carries 50% of the marks for this paper.

- The mark scheme for this exam divides marks between the Assessment Objectives as follows:

Assessment Objective	% of marks
AO1: Critical interpretation and textual support	35%
AO2: Language analysis	35%
AO3: Understanding of context	20%
AO4: Vocabulary, Sentences, Spelling and Punctuation	10%

Set texts

You will be studying ONE of the following:

Macbeth   *Romeo and Juliet*

The Merchant of Venice   *Much Ado About Nothing*

Questions will be based on characters and their relationships to each other, to the events of the play and to its themes. They will also require you to explore Shakespeare's language, imagery and use of dramatic form by looking closely at details of the writing.

Quotation Bank

Throughout the chapter, you will be encouraged to assemble a quote bank on key characters in the play you are studying. You will need to concentrate on key scenes and explore their language in detail. You will be encouraged to link characters to key debates about the meaning of the plays.

However, it is also a good idea to explore key words in order to unlock the meaning of a Shakespeare play. Shakespeare often used particular words many times and in different forms in order to emphasise what mattered most in a play. Word searches are easy as Shakespeare texts are easily available in searchable online versions.

Activity

Search and bank quotations with the following key words for each of your set texts:

- *Macbeth*: 'blood'
- *Romeo and Juliet*: 'stars'
- *Much Ado About Nothing*: 'wit'
- *The Merchant of Venice*: 'bond'

You may need to refine your 'Advanced Search' to the exact word, or you will have too many!

1. What do these words tell you about the meaning of the play?

2. Can you already see a 'development' or 'journey' within the play as it goes on?

3. Which characters use these words the most and what does that tell you about them?

Unit 1 How do you study Shakespeare?

Learning objectives

- To revise knowledge of Shakespeare's plays and verse

- To explore Shakespeare's use of form and structure

- To appreciate the genres of tragedy and comedy

Reintroducing Shakespeare

Shakespeare's plays and poetry remain at the heart of studying English Literature. You have probably read and perhaps performed a Shakespeare play during years 7 to 9, and you may already have written essays on his plays. Why do we study this dramatist whose plays belong on the stage?

In his own time, Shakespeare achieved fame and fortune not as a writer but as an actor-manager, producing scripts for live performance. Ben Jonson, his friend and competitor, called him:

Soul of the age!
The applause, delight, the wonder of our stage!

The stage is where Shakespeare belongs. Shakespeare's characters and plots are compelling enough to have been adapted into musicals and Hollywood films. They are popular all over the world. You probably know quite a lot about Shakespeare's theatre, and may even have visited a replica theatre. It was difficult for audiences to see the action. They talked about going to 'hear' a play, which shows how important the words were. We need to understand Shakespeare's words to 'hear' the plays today.

You study Shakespeare by reading and appreciating:

- the form and structure of his plays

- the language his characters use

- how drama affects the audience

- your own reaction to the play and its themes.

Think about how important each of these is and keep notes on each of these points as you study your set text.

Activity 1

Discuss the questions below and then look up the facts online.

1. Which Shakespeare plays can you name?

2. Which two well-known theatre companies specialize in performing Shakespeare's works?

3. Which well-known Hollywood actors have appeared in Shakespearean roles?

4. Which theatres performed Shakespeare's plays in his own lifetime? In what ways did Shakespeare's theatres differ from theatres today?

Stretch

Think of a Shakespeare play that has been adapted into a musical or film.

1. What changes were made?

2. What do these suggest about our continuing interest in the story?

Shakespeare the poet

To appreciate your GCSE set text, it helps to understand Shakespeare as a poet. Actors use Shakespeare's sonnets in order to get used to his unusual but memorable language, his use of imagery (especially metaphors) and his use of poetic rhythms and forms. You can use your 'poetry toolkit' to interpret the sonnets, and that will help you to appreciate the verse of your set play.

Sonnets are mini-dramas: a problem is laid out and followed by a solution. You can see the ending coming, but it might not give you all the answers. The following poem is about love, the key theme in Shakespeare's comedies, but also time and fate (tragic themes):

Source text A

Sonnet 18: 'Shall I compare thee to a summer's day?'

Shall I compare thee to a summer's day?
Thou art more lovely and more temperate:
Rough winds do shake the darling buds of May,
And summer's lease hath all too short a date;

Sometime too hot the eye of heaven shines,
And often is his gold complexion dimm'd;
And every fair from fair sometime declines,
By chance or nature's changing course untrimm'd;

But thy eternal summer shall not fade
Nor lose possession of that fair thou ow'st;
Nor shall death brag thou wander'st in his shade,
When in eternal lines to time thou grow'st:

So long as men can breathe or eyes can see,
So long lives this and this gives life to thee.

First **quatrain**. Why is the beloved better than a summer's day? Where do the strong stresses – or beats – fall in line 3? Shakespeare uses **iambic pentameters** in his sonnets, just like the plays.

Second quatrain – development. What qualities does the day have in common with the beloved? How does Shakespeare use **end-stopping** to mark the end of the day? The first eight lines make up an octave.

Why is there **enjambment** at the end of line 9?

Who is personified? Who is addressed?

Shakespeare ends with a **rhyming couplet** which acts as a kind of conclusion. Sometimes he introduces a new idea here. What gives eternal life to the beloved 'thou'? Who or what is the subject of these lines?

There is a change of subject and rhyme scheme (a volta) at the third quatrain. What or who is now the subject of these lines?

Key terms

Quatrain a four-line section of verse

Iambic pentameter the five-beat line made up of unstressed and stressed syllables which Shakespeare uses most frequently in his plays; when unrhymed, this is called blank verse

End-stopping use of punctuation at the end of a line

Enjambment a run-on line with no punctuation which should be read without pausing

Rhyming couplet a pair of lines in which the final stressed syllables rhyme

Activity 2

Now you have read the poem, what do you think it says about love and about what can survive time and death?

Key themes in Shakespeare's work

Shakespeare's poetry is what lives on. Let's use Sonnet 18, on page 135, to explore some of the key themes in Shakespeare plays.

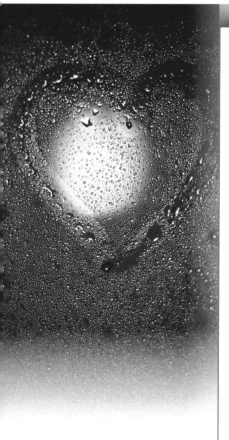

Activity 3

Love

Many of Shakespeare's plays are about lovers, both younger and older lovers.

1. Which Shakespeare characters can you name who are in love?
2. Which love affairs end happily? Which end less happily?
3. Does age make a difference?
4. How can you tell the first quatrain of the poem is about a young person?

Change

Shakespeare also described the 'Seven Ages of Man'. Chance and time ('nature's changing course untrimm'd') inevitably bring changes.

1. Which age of man does this poem refer to?
2. Which season does Shakespeare associate with love?
3. What changes occur in the plays you have studied? For better or for worse?
4. Did characters' choices make a difference?

Death and immortality

Death is the ultimate change and is personified in the third quatrain of the poem. But Shakespeare suggests that 'eternal lines' of poetry can survive even death.

1. Which characters needed to risk or confront death?
2. Did they survive or not?
3. Which were the famous lines in the plays that you can still remember?

Conclusion

Sonnets conclude neatly with a rhyming couplet. The ending of the play depends on its **genre**: comedies usually end in marriage, tragedies in multiple deaths, while history plays keep moving on.

1. How did your plays end?
2. Were you satisfied with the ending? Like a drama, the sonnet has a striking opening, raising questions. It develops, with different twists and turns, and it clearly ends.

Key term

Genre the form of a literary text, such as a tragedy or comedy

Shakespeare the tragedian

Romeo and Juliet

Shakespeare's most famous love story is a **tragedy**: *Romeo and Juliet*. Shakespeare wanted his audience to be aware of the influence of fate, so they could appreciate the **irony** of the drama. Most of Shakespeare's plays were based on well-known plots (or stories) so the audience would have known what was coming, creating **dramatic irony**.

Romeo and Juliet is based on the love story of Pyramus and Thisbe. It has all the ingredients of a **comedy**: young couples, quarrels, fooling, poetry and music. However, after the first death in the play, which is an accident, the atmosphere immediately darkens.

Now read this prologue, which alerts the audience to the fate of the characters. It's another sonnet.

Source text B

Romeo and Juliet

Two households, both alike in dignity,
In fair Verona, (where we lay our scene),
From ancient grudge break to new mutiny,
Where civil blood makes civil hands unclean.

From forth the fatal loins of these two foes
A pair of star-cross'd lovers take their life;
Whose misadventur'd piteous overthrows
Doth with their death bury their parents' strife.

The fearful passage of their death-mark'd love,
And the continuance of their parents' rage,
Which, but their children's end, nought could remove,
Is now the two hours' traffic of our stage;

The which if you with patient ears attend,
What here shall miss, our toil shall strive to mend.

Key terms

Tragedy a play that stimulates pity and fear in the audience, as it shows the characters at the mercy of fate

Irony when the surface meaning is opposite to the intended meaning, like sarcasm, but when nobody is insulted

Dramatic irony when the audience is aware of something inevitable that is about to happen, unknown to the characters.

Comedy a play that provokes an audience to laugh, which has a happy ending, with characters reconciled, or even married

Activity 4

Explore the prologue as a sonnet.

1. Which quatrain explains the problems between the Montagues and Capulets? Pick out the words which give contrasting images of the beauty and nastiness of Verona.

2. Where does Shakespeare give the plot away? Which words suggest Romeo and Juliet are victims? What is the effect of their deaths?

3. Why do you think he addresses the audience in the couplet? What did the work of actors need to 'mend' or make up for in the theatre of his day?

Stretch

Find other sonnets in *Romeo and Juliet*. One of them occurs when the lovers first meet. What is the effect of this sonnet?

Macbeth

SCENE I. The battlefield.

Thunder and lightning. Enter three Witches

First Witch

When shall we three meet again?
In thunder, lightning, or in rain?

Second Witch

When the hurly-burly's done,
When the battle's lost and won.

Third Witch

That will be ere the set of sun.

First Witch

Where the place?

Second Witch

Upon the heath.

Third Witch

There to meet with Macbeth.

[…]

ALL

Fair is foul, and foul is fair,
Hover through the fog
and filthy air. *Exeunt*

Macbeth

Shakespeare's *Macbeth*, a later play, is experimental in its use of rhyme and its presentation of fate. The Witches, or 'weird sisters', embody fate, and its twists and surprises. What does this suggest about the fate of Macbeth?

Activity 5

1. Read aloud the scene of *Macbeth* so you can hear the rhythms of the verse.

2. Compare the rhythms and sounds you hear to the iambic pentameters of the sonnets.

3. What have you found disturbing and shocking about this opening?

Shakespeare the comedian

Comedies need to end happily, but they are also based around problems, ironies and misunderstandings. Think about the Shakespeare comedies you know already.

- What caused misunderstandings or made you laugh?

- Why might things have ended badly?

- How did the play come to end happily?

Comedies depend on double acts and partnerships. Shakespeare's comedies quickly introduce friendship groups, rivalries and problems. We also quickly identify who the potential lovers are. As in *Romeo and Juliet*, young men and women lived very different lives, so it is often a problem to get them together.

Much Ado About Nothing

Much Ado About Nothing is a comedy, and ends with marriages. But the 'war of wit' between Beatrice and Benedick, which begins the play, establishes the mood for the audience. There are references to wars and rebellion throughout this play. The comedy almost turns to tragedy for the lovers, Hero and Claudio. Most of the laughs come from Beatrice and Benedick, who are brought together by a joke.

Like Macbeth, Benedick is a character we hear about before he appears. What is the effect of this on an audience?

Source text D

Much Ado About Nothing

BEATRICE

I pray you, is Signior Montanto returned from the wars or no?

Messenger

I know none of that name, lady. There was none such in the army, of any sort.

LEONATO

What is he that you ask for, niece?

HERO

My cousin means Signior Benedick of Padua.

Messenger

O, he's returned, and as pleasant as ever he was.

BEATRICE

He set up his bills here in Messina, and challenged Cupid at the flight; and my uncle's fool, reading the challenge, subscribed for Cupid, and challenged him at the bird-bolt. I pray you, how many hath he killed and eaten in these wars? But how many hath he killed? For indeed I promised to eat all of his killing.

LEONATO

Faith, niece, you tax Signior Benedick too much. But he'll be meet with you, I doubt it not.

Messenger

He hath done good service, lady, in these wars.

Act out the extract from *Much Ado About Nothing*, on page 139.

1. Which words did the actor playing Beatrice stress to bring out her sarcasm?
2. How did the messenger bring out his view of Benedick?
3. How is Leonato's character and sense of humour established?
4. What do we now know about Beatrice and Benedick?

The Merchant of Venice

Risky business, in love and money, is the theme of *The Merchant of Venice*. A young man, Bassanio, can hit the jackpot if he can attract Portia, a young woman who has been left plenty of money ('richly left') as well as being beautiful ('fair'). But to do that he must borrow more money from his friend, the merchant Antonio, who will have to borrow it himself, as he has put his own money into risky investments.

Source text E

The Merchant of Venice

BASSANIO

In Belmont is a lady richly left,
And she is fair, and—fairer than that word—
Of wondrous virtues. Sometimes from her eyes
I did receive fair speechless messages.
Her name is Portia, nothing undervalued
To Cato's daughter, Brutus' Portia.
Nor is the wide world ignorant of her worth;
For the four winds blow in from every coast
Renowned suitors, and her sunny locks
Hang on her temples like a golden fleece,
Which makes her seat of Belmont Colchos' strand,
And many Jasons come in quest of her.
O my Antonio, had I but the means
To hold a rival place with one of them,
I have a mind presages me such thrift
That I should questionless be fortunate.

Activity 7

1. Find the words in the extract that we might associate with beauty.

2. Find the words associated with money.

3. Explain Bassanio's problem.

4. What will be Portia's problem if she falls for him?

Stretch

Shakespeare's comedies often use complex **allusions**. Find out what you can about Jason and the Golden Fleece. How does the allusion illustrate the problems behind the play?

Key term

Allusion a reference to another text, legend, or historical event for the purpose of comparison

Activity 8

Begin your notes on your Shakespeare play by considering how the first scenes set it up. Copy and complete the following table.

	Your comments on the scene	Provide evidence with a short quotation	Comment on what the quotation shows the audience
How the *genre* is introduced			
How *characters* are introduced through language			
How *relationships* between characters are introduced			
How *problems* are introduced for the audience			

Unit 2 Understanding context

Learning objectives

- To explore how context affects meaning
- To understand how Shakespeare's drama differed from ours
- To analyse the world the plays present to us, and how to interpret it

Key term

Context the setting or circumstances of when a text was written

What is context?

Context is what surrounds the text, the words or passages we are studying. We use this term in two main ways, both important in literature studies. The literary context of a word or passage is how it relates to the rest of the text. The social and historical context of a word or passage is the way it relates to the time when it was written, or how we interpret that context today. In the Shakespeare essay, you will be assessed on literary context (AO1) and social, historical and theatrical context (AO3).

Exam link

The GCSE exam asks you to study Shakespeare and the 19th-century novel in relation to their contexts. Assessment Objective 3 states: show understanding of the relationship between texts and the contexts in which they were written.

The most important context for Shakespeare's plays was his theatre, and the audience who would have 'heard' the play. Nevertheless, to understand that audience and how it is affected by his writing we need to know how their world differed from ours today.

Activity 1

First, explore some dates and details. Copy and complete this timeline with the date your set text was written, along with as many dates as you can find for other well-known plays and historical events of the time. Most of the dates given for plays are good guesses, not facts!

1564 Shakespeare born in Stratford-upon-Avon

1592 first critical mention of Shakespeare

1603 Queen Elizabeth dies, James I and VI becomes King of England as well as Scotland

1610 *The Tempest:* last play Shakespeare wrote on his own

1588 Spanish Armada defeated

1599 Shakespeare's theatre company moves to The Globe

1605 *King Lear*

1616 Shakespeare's death

Shakespeare and kingship

Leadership and hierarchy were obviously important to Shakespeare and his audience. The titles of his plays tell you that. Plays without kings are dominated by princes and counts. Rulers mattered in Shakespeare's time. London was dominated by the Royal Court, as well as trade and the City. By the time of *Macbeth*, the childless Elizabeth I had been succeeded by the King of Scotland. James and his sons enjoyed theatre, especially stories of Greece and Rome. Shakespeare's theatre company was now called 'The King's Men' and performed at court, as well as at The Globe. Shakespeare was a 'sharer' or shareholder of the company.

A play about a Scottish king would be popular, and James I had a personal interest in witchcraft, even writing a book on the subject. However, Shakespeare was on dangerous territory when writing about the murder of a king (many of James's ancestors had been murdered and James himself feared assassination). The play dangerously suggests there are powers of fate stronger than earthly powers. Shakespeare gets round this by presenting Banquo, James I's ancestor, favourably, as a **foil** to Macbeth.

James also believed in the Divine Right of Kings, that kings were ordained by God and by destiny. Most people in Shakespeare's time believed that your destiny or fate had already been decided; they were highly religious.

Given this context, consider why this exchange between Macbeth and Banquo at the beginning of the play would be so shocking. What does it suggest to you about hierarchy, succession, fate and evil?

Key term

Foil a contrasting character who brings out opposite qualities to his or her counterpart, for example, Banquo's conscience contrasts with Macbeth's ambition

Source text A

Macbeth

MACBETH

[Aside] Glamis, and Thane of Cawdor:
The greatest is behind.–Thanks for your pains.—

[To BANQUO]

Do you not hope your children shall be kings,
When those that gave the Thane of Cawdor to me
Promis'd no less to them?

BANQUO

   That trusted home,
Might yet enkindle you unto the crown,
Besides the Thane of Cawdor. But 'tis strange,
And oftentimes, to win us to our harm,
The instruments of darkness tell us truths;
Win us with honest trifles, to betray's
In deepest consequence.–
Cousins, a word, I pray you.

MACBETH

[Aside] Two truths are told,
As happy prologues to the swelling act
Of the imperial theme.–I thank you, gentlemen.—

This supernatural soliciting
Cannot be ill, cannot be good. If ill,
Why hath it given me earnest of success,
Commencing in a truth? I am Thane of Cawdor.
If good, why do I yield to that suggestion,
Whose horrid image doth unfix my hair
And make my seated heart knock at my ribs
Against the use of nature? Present fears
Are less than horrible imaginings.
My thought, whose murder yet is but fantastical,
Shakes so my single state of man that function
Is smother'd in surmise, and nothing is
But what is not.

Activity 2

Imagine you are Banquo at this moment. Write a letter to Fleance, your son. What do you think of what the witches said, and of Macbeth's reaction?

Activity 3

Explore the hierarchy of your play. In the following plays, consider:

- *Macbeth:* the royal family and thanes
- *Romeo and Juliet:* the families and gangs and the role of the Prince
- *Much Ado About Nothing:* Don Pedro, families, and servants
- *The Merchant of Venice:* the ranks of different people in Belmont and Venice.

With a partner, draw up a set of character trees. Organize your charts so that the most important families are at the top, and the servants at the bottom.

Stretch

Find out more about any of the following contextual topics:

- fate and predestination: what Shakespeare's audience believed
- why family values are important in your play
- Shakespeare's King and Queen: why were they controversial figures?
- religious belief and superstition
- censorship in Renaissance theatre.

Present a short piece to the class and answer questions about your topic.

Shakespeare and the family

Questions of succession were important to all families, not just the royal family. In Shakespeare's time, eldest sons inherited most of the family property, although settlements were made for other children. When girls married, they ceased to be the 'property' of their father and became the 'property' of their husbands. It was difficult for women to own much in their own right. Marriages in rich or powerful families were usually arranged, often at an early age. Shakespeare's audience would be less shocked than us by Lady Capulet's attitudes or the will of Portia's father.

The children of wealthy women were 'nursed' (breastfed) by servants, and girls educated by servants. They often grew up closer to their servants than their parents. The father or ward of an only daughter would be expected to pay a large dowry (sum of money) to her husband. How does this influence the lives of Juliet, Portia, Hero and Beatrice?

Source text B

Source text B

Romeo and Juliet

LADY CAPULET

Well, think of marriage now; younger than you,
Here in Verona, ladies of esteem,
Are made already mothers. By my count,
I was your mother much upon these years
That you are now a maid. Thus then in brief:
The valiant Paris seeks you for his love.

Nurse

A man, young lady! lady, such a man
As all the world–why, he's a man of wax.

LADY CAPULET

Verona's summer hath not such a flower.

Nurse

Nay, he's a flower, in faith, a very flower.

LADY CAPULET

What say you? Can you love the gentleman?
This night you shall behold him at our feast;
Read o'er the volume of young Paris' face,
And find delight writ there with beauty's pen;
Examine every married lineament,
And see how one another lends content;
And what obscur'd in this fair volume lies
Find written in the margent of his eyes.
This precious book of love, this unbound lover,
To beautify him, only lacks a cover.
The fish lives in the sea, and 'tis much pride
For fair without the fair within to hide;
That book in many's eyes doth share the glory
That in gold clasps locks in the golden story:
So shall you share all that he doth possess,
By having him, making yourself no less.

Activity 4

1. What does the line, 'So shall you share all that he doth possess' suggest about Lady Capulet's attitude to the potential marriage?

2. How does that attitude link to the social context of wealthy women's lives in Shakespeare's time?

3. Write a short explanation of how a Renaissance audience would react to one of the following:

   • Romeo and Juliet's relationships with their parents

   • Bassanio's relationship with Antonio

   • Beatrice's place in Leonato's family

   • The childless marriage of Macbeth and Lady Macbeth.

Stretch

1. How does the verse change when Lady Capulet begins to talk about love?

2. What does this suggest about how conventional her ideas about love are?

Shakespeare and women

We have seen how men and women lived different lives. Men like Macbeth and Benedick went to war. Lady Capulet and Lady Macbeth stayed at home, forming different plots and schemes. In the following scene, notice that Benedick speaks in prose, despite his high birth. This shows how differently he feels about love. It also suggests that the audience might not take him, or his offensive views about women, too seriously.

Source text C

Much Ado About Nothing

BENEDICK

That a woman conceived me, I thank her. That she brought me up, I likewise give her most humble thanks. But that I will have a recheat winded in my forehead, or hang my bugle in an invisible baldric, all women shall pardon me. Because I will not do them the wrong to mistrust any, I will do myself the right to trust none. And the fine is—for the which I may go the finer—I will live a bachelor.

DON PEDRO

I shall see thee ere I die look pale with love.

BENEDICK

With anger, with sickness, or with hunger, my lord; not with love. Prove that ever I lose more blood with love than I will get again with drinking, pick out mine eyes with a ballad-maker's pen and hang me up at the door of a brothel house for the sign of blind Cupid.

DON PEDRO

Well, if ever thou dost fall from this faith thou wilt prove a notable argument.

Benedick's language suggests how he might spend his leisure time: he refers to bull-baiting, shooting contests, brothels, drinking and hunting. All these activities were available to young men not far from Shakespeare's theatre, beyond the City gates.

Activity 5

How are relations between men and women portrayed in the early scenes of your set text? Write some contextual notes for your play on how Shakespeare's audience would have understood:

- *Romeo and Juliet:* Romeo's gang versus Juliet's isolation
- *Macbeth:* Macbeth's military record compared with how Lady Macbeth is expected to behave
- *The Merchant of Venice:* The behaviour and language of Bassanio's friends compared to the more feminine world of Belmont
- *Much Ado About Nothing:* Benedick's banter versus Hero's shyness.

Shakespeare and different cultures

We saw how Shakespeare's world regarded outsiders at the beginning of *The Merchant of Venice*. There are two characters outside the circles of love and relationships: they are Antonio and Shylock, and they hate each other. Both are obsessed with trade and making money. Antonio likes to give his money away; Shylock lends it, profiting from the interest he charges.

Shakespeare's London had many inhabitants of different races and religions, as it was a centre of trade. However, anyone who did not share the state religion, Anglicanism, was regarded with deep suspicion. There were many arguments about how the Bible should be interpreted, but the traditional view was that the Christian Bible prohibited usury, that is, borrowing money and charging interest.

Catholic Italians would have taken Antonio's side in this argument. However, Shakespeare's London was a Protestant city, and there was a lot of argument about charging interest. If banks could profit from their lending, they were more likely to fund a risky venture. London merchants would be interested in Shylock's arguments. Notice that Antonio uses the word 'venture' and Shylock uses the word 'thrift'. What do these words mean and suggest about their attitudes?

Read the extract from *The Merchant of Venice* on page 148 to explore this further.

The Merchant of Venice

SHYLOCK

When Jacob graz'd his uncle Laban's sheep–
This Jacob from our holy Abram was
(As his wise mother wrought in his behalf)
The third possessor; ay, he was the third–

ANTONIO

And what of him, did he take interest?

SHYLOCK

No, not take interest, not as you would say
Directly interest. Mark what Jacob did:
When Laban and himself were compromis'd
That all the eanlings which were streak'd and pied
Should fall as Jacob's hire, the ewes being rank,
In the end of autumn turned to the rams,
And when the work of generation was
Between these woolly breeders in the act,
The skilful shepherd pill'd me certain wands
And in the doing of the deed of kind
He stuck them up before the fulsome ewes,
Who then conceiving, did in eaning time
Fall parti-coloured lambs, and those were Jacob's.
This was a way to thrive, and he was blest;
And thrift is blessing if men steal it not.

ANTONIO

This was a venture, sir, that Jacob serv'd for,
A thing not in his power to bring to pass,
But sway'd and fashion'd by the hand of heaven.
Was this inserted to make interest good?
Or is your gold and silver ewes and rams?

SHYLOCK

I cannot tell, I make it breed as fast.

> Why is this story from the Bible important to Jews?

> What was the name Christians gave to charging interest and what did they believe happened in the after-life to those who did it?

> Why would Shakespeare's audience find these lines funny?

> How has Jacob increased his profit? What lesson does Shylock think the story teaches?

> What does Shylock mean by 'thrift'?

> Do you think Shylock's joke helps him win the argument?

To understand *The Merchant of Venice* today, audiences need a note on usury, and an explanation of how Shylock's Jewishness is portrayed. Why does he argue about the interpretation of the sacred text? Why does Antonio say 'the devil can cite Scripture'? Shakespeare's audience were very familiar with the Bible: they were fined if they did not go to church. What needs to be explained about this passage today? How would answering the questions in the notes help a modern director perform these difficult lines better?

Today, theatre audiences usually have a programme to explain who is who in the play and how they are connected. It might also include short essays on important context for the play.

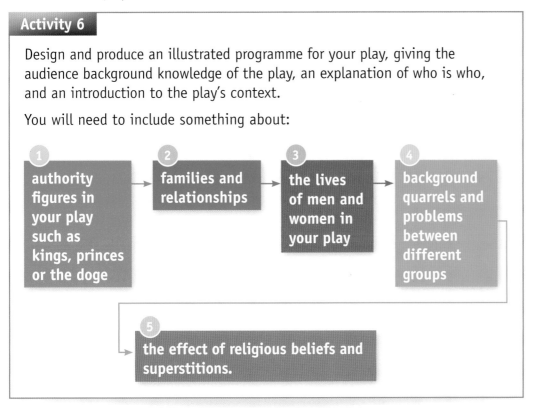

Activity 6

Design and produce an illustrated programme for your play, giving the audience background knowledge of the play, an explanation of who is who, and an introduction to the play's context.

You will need to include something about:

1. authority figures in your play such as kings, princes or the doge
2. families and relationships
3. the lives of men and women in your play
4. background quarrels and problems between different groups
5. the effect of religious beliefs and superstitions.

Once you have the context of the world the characters live in, and how Shakespeare's audience would have understood it, you are ready to examine the main characters in more detail.

Unit 3 Exploring meaning

Learning objectives

- To look for meaning in passages that develop characters
- To connect characters to different readings of the text

Learning objectives

- To look for meaning in passages that develop characters
- To connect characters to different readings of the text

Exam link

A01 requires you to read, understand and respond to texts. You need to be able to use textual references, including quotations, to support and illustrate interpretations.

This is assessed in your Shakespeare essay through exploration of characters, supported by detail. You should respond to different ways audiences might see characters and their relationships.

Key term

Empathy our ability to relate to the emotions of someone else

Characters in Shakespeare

Shakespeare is famous for the characters he created. Actors love playing them and audiences respond to them with laughter or **empathy**. Successful characters need to combine realistic attributes with the ability to use language in striking ways; they are recognizable but also unusual.

Activity 1

1. List the main characters in the play you are studying.

2. Work in small groups on different characters. Some should identify the realistic elements of their chosen character. Others can list what makes him or her unusual or different. Use adjectives to describe them.

3. What are the memorable things your character says? What is said about him or her? Add to your quote bank.

4. Present to your group what makes your character striking and memorable.

Developing characters through their speeches

It is not just main characters who contribute to the audience's experience. Take Mercutio in *Romeo and Juliet*. He makes a memorable impact on stage and in film versions. He is funny, quick-witted and brings Romeo to the party where he meets Juliet. But he has a cynical attitude about love and Romeo never tells him about Juliet; this has tragic consequences. Sharp-tongued Mercutio won't back down when defending himself or his friends. His death darkens the play, moving it from comedy to tragedy.

You can easily identify him as a joker but he stops the show with a long and complex speech.

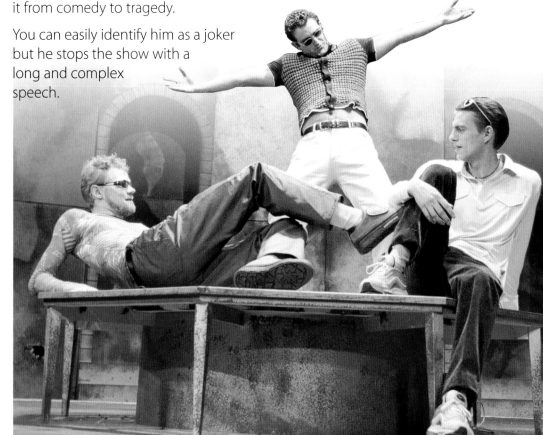

Source text A

Romeo and Juliet

MERCUTIO

O then I see Queen Mab hath been with you:
She is the fairies' midwife, and she comes
In shape no bigger than an agate-stone
On the forefinger of an alderman,
Drawn with a team of little atomi
Over men's noses as they lie asleep.
Her chariot is an empty hazel-nut,
Made by the joiner squirrel or old grub,
Time out o'mind the fairies' coachmakers:
[....]

And in this state she gallops night by night
Through lovers' brains, and then they dream of love,
O'er courtiers' knees, that dream on cur'sies straight,
O'er lawyers' fingers, who straight dream on fees,
O'er ladies' lips, who straight on kisses dream,
Which oft the angry Mab with blisters plagues,
Because their breaths with sweetmeats tainted are.
Sometime she gallops o'er a courtier's nose,
And then dreams he of smelling out a suit;
[....]

... This is that very Mab
That plats the manes of horses in the night,
And bakes the elf-locks in foul sluttish hairs,
Which once untangl'd, much misfortune bodes.
This is the hag, when maids lie on their backs,
That presses them and learns them first to bear,
Making them women of good carriage.
This is she–

ROMEO

      Peace, peace, Mercutio, peace!
Thou talk'st of nothing.

MERCUTIO

      True, I talk of dreams,
Which are the children of an idle brain,
Begot of nothing but vain fantasy, [...]

Mercutio's idea of Queen Mab links her with birth – rather like the Nurse – but the births she attends are imaginary.

Mercutio's images present the tiny fairy world which Shakespeare also introduced in A Midsummer Night's Dream.

Nature is linked to human work and occupations.

Enjambment speeds up the pace here.

Now the theme is clearly love and dreams.

Not all the dreams are innocent.

And Mab is mischievous like most fairies.

The dreams of older people have more to do with money and power, or destruction and violence.

Mab is also responsible for bad omens.

Or for teenage pregnancies – after all she is a midwife.

There's a pun on carriage: the fairy has her own carriage but women bear children, if they have paid too much attention to their dreams.

Why does Romeo tell Mercutio to calm down?

Notice how Mercutio completes Romeo's line: why are dreams 'nothing'?

Mercutio's metaphors are again about childbirth.

In Baz Luhrmann's film, Mercutio's speech is brilliantly and disturbingly delivered, as he gives Romeo a drug before the Capulet's party. Why do you think he cross dresses in Luhrmann's version? How does this fit the imagery of the speech?

> ## Activity 2
>
> Is there a long speech in your set text that defines a character you are interested in?
>
> 1. Find the speech and turn it into a poster.
> 2. Illustrate your poster with a striking image of the character.
> 3. Use annotation to explain difficult language and suggest what it shows about your character.

Characters and controversy

The most interesting characters are three-dimensional and full of contradictions. Lady Macbeth is another character with dreams and premonitions, closely linked to fate and tragedy. At times in the play she seems supernaturally harsh and inhuman, more like the witches than a human being. However, her human side emerges as the play progresses: she would not kill Duncan because he resembled her father as he slept; she faints at talk about the bloody daggers; Macbeth does not involve her in his later murders; and her guilt emerges in the 'sleepwalking scene'.

> ## Activity 3
>
> Who is the most controversial character in your play? Consider characters such as Bassanio, Beatrice and Benedick, as well as more obvious 'villains'.
>
> 1. Interview them, or put them in the 'hot seat' to answer your questions.
> 2. Write this up as a magazine profile for 'Celebrities At Home'. What does your character really like? What do people say about them? What do they say?
> 3. Build up your quote bank by finding textual support for your points.

Lady Macbeth is a terrifying character because she is realistic, with disturbingly strong and excitable feelings, and can conjure up powerful images through her language.

When Shakespeare writes about the supernatural, there are always links to what we now call psychology. In context, Shakespeare's audience were more superstitious than people today. However, they knew poetry used imagery to convey a state of mind. Like Mercutio, Lady Macbeth appeals to dreams and nightmares. Is she as evil as she pretends?

In this annotated speech, Lady Macbeth seems to invoke powers of darkness to help her persuade Macbeth. She is talking in a **soliloquy**.

Source text B

Macbeth

LADY MACBETH

Come, you spirits
That tend on mortal thoughts, unsex me here
And fill me from the crown to the toe topfull
Of direst cruelty; make thick my blood,
Stop up th'access and passage to remorse
That no compunctious visitings of nature
Shake my fell purpose nor keep peace between
Th'effect and it. Come to my woman's breasts
And take my milk for gall, you murd'ring ministers,
Wherever in your sightless substances
You wait on nature's mischief. Come, thick night,
And pall thee in the dunnest smoke of hell,
That my keen knife see not the wound it makes,
Nor heaven peep through the blanket of the dark,
To cry, 'Hold, hold!'

> Who is she speaking to? Where does she say these spirits come from?

> Why would nature be an enemy?

> Where else are there suggestions that Macbeth and Lady Macbeth have no child, or lost a child?

> Which sound effects invoke the thick darkness of the night?

> More images of darkness.

> Notice she would like murder to be invisible. Why is this idea important later?

Characters and their fate

We will now look at another notorious character. Shylock causes much controversy among audiences, especially today. If you focus on his tragedy, you will pity him. Treat the play as a comedy and see him in context, rather than be influenced by recent history, and you might judge him differently. Look at his language used on page 154.

Activity 4

The most interesting characters in a play are those you can have a debate about. Are they good or bad? Are they to blame for what goes wrong?

1. Choose a character (or several characters) from the play you are studying, for example, Bassanio, Macbeth, the Nurse, Claudio.

2. Agree on a 'motion' – a statement – to describe this character in an extreme way, whether positive or negative. This is called 'parliamentary' debate.

3. Look for evidence for and against the motion and draw conclusions as to whether you agree or disagree. Discuss your thoughts with a partner.

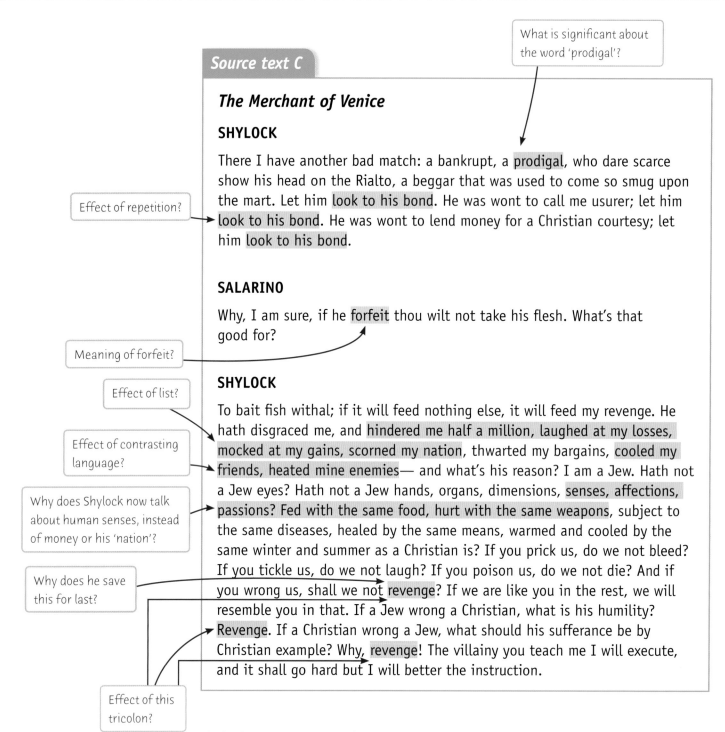

Source text C

The Merchant of Venice

SHYLOCK

There I have another bad match: a bankrupt, a prodigal, who dare scarce show his head on the Rialto, a beggar that was used to come so smug upon the mart. Let him look to his bond. He was wont to call me usurer; let him look to his bond. He was wont to lend money for a Christian courtesy; let him look to his bond.

SALARINO

Why, I am sure, if he forfeit thou wilt not take his flesh. What's that good for?

SHYLOCK

To bait fish withal; if it will feed nothing else, it will feed my revenge. He hath disgraced me, and hindered me half a million, laughed at my losses, mocked at my gains, scorned my nation, thwarted my bargains, cooled my friends, heated mine enemies— and what's his reason? I am a Jew. Hath not a Jew eyes? Hath not a Jew hands, organs, dimensions, senses, affections, passions? Fed with the same food, hurt with the same weapons, subject to the same diseases, healed by the same means, warmed and cooled by the same winter and summer as a Christian is? If you prick us, do we not bleed? If you tickle us, do we not laugh? If you poison us, do we not die? And if you wrong us, shall we not revenge? If we are like you in the rest, we will resemble you in that. If a Jew wrong a Christian, what is his humility? Revenge. If a Christian wrong a Jew, what should his sufferance be by Christian example? Why, revenge! The villainy you teach me I will execute, and it shall go hard but I will better the instruction.

Margin annotations:

- What is significant about the word 'prodigal'?
- Effect of repetition?
- Meaning of forfeit?
- Effect of list?
- Effect of contrasting language?
- Why does Shylock now talk about human senses, instead of money or his 'nation'?
- Why does he save this for last?
- Effect of this tricolon?

Shylock wants revenge after Antonio's friends helped Jessica to elope. In tragedy, we have seen that events are often governed by fate. In comedy, by contrast, characters often make choices or take actions to prevent tragedy. Is Shylock a victim of fate, or of his own choices? Does Shakespeare help us to see things from his point of view, or criticize his attitudes? As characters develop, we find them more complicated.

Activity 5

Is the characters' fate and **development** presented as their choice or destiny?

Look back over your play so far and find evidence for the two columns in the table below.

Fate	Choice
Antonio's fortune depends on the seas	But he chooses to lend money to Bassanio
Portia's fate is to marry the man who solves the riddle	But the riddle is based on a man making the right choice – and he gets some help from Portia
Jessica?	
Bassanio?	

Can you apply a similar framework to Shylock, Macbeth, Romeo, Juliet, Hero or Claudio? Are they victims? Or have they made bad choices?

Key term

Development the way a character or text moves on and changes, showing different dimensions

Activity 6

Shakespeare rarely presents even his heroes as wholly good. As in real life, we need to balance strengths and weaknesses.

1. Are the characters you are studying villains or victims? Or a bit of both?

2. Even the 'good' characters have their flaws. Do their good qualities really outbalance their bad ones?

3. Add evidence to your quote bank *for* and *against* your main characters.

Unit 4 Analysing language

Language in Shakespeare

Language reveals how characters develop and change, and an audience's reactions change with them.

When you write about extracts in the exam, you should comment on dramatic context as well as their cultural context. You must make links to other parts of the play. Chart the 'journey' of characters in your text by identifying *key scenes* where we see changes in their attitudes or behaviour.

Activity 1

Make a table listing your play's main characters and identify three turning points when each character develops or changes. Can you find a speech or short extract to show that change? Add Act and Scene references to the box.

Name of main character	Where is the character introduced?	Where do we find out more about them?	Where do they surprise or shock us?	Where do they recognize they have changed?

When a character has secrets, or is struggling to make a choice, Shakespeare often has them speak their thoughts directly to the audience, in soliloquy. After Macbeth has killed King Duncan, he changes. At first he is frightened and guilty, and dependent on Lady Macbeth. Once crowned King, however, he decides further murders will make his position secure. Macbeth reveals his plans about Banquo to us, and not to Lady Macbeth. It is an early sign that the murder of Duncan is driving them apart. This soliloquy focuses on his feelings about Banquo, no longer a friend but a dangerous rival who knows too much.

Look at the extract opposite. On first reading, look out for nouns, such as *royalty, temper, wisdom, genius, kings, crown, sceptre, jewel*. They give you the subject of the speech: it is about royalty and succession.

On second reading, pay attention to adjectives. These descriptive words give you the emotions expressed: they include *dauntless* (describing Banquo), *fruitless, barren, unlineal* (describing the crown). How do these suggest that Macbeth is worried about his former friend and about his own kingship?

Key terms

Metaphor when a writer describes something as if it *is* something else

Personification when a writer gives an inhuman thing human qualities, for example, 'The tree waved its arms in the wind'

What does Macbeth's description of Banquo suggest about his own royalty?

Source text A

The 'royal we'

Macbeth

To be thus is nothing,
But to be safely thus. Our fears in Banquo
Stick deep, and in his royalty of nature
Reigns that which would be fear'd. 'Tis much he dares,
And to that dauntless temper of his mind,
He hath a wisdom that doth guide his valour
To act in safety. There is none but he,
Whose being I do fear; and under him.
My genius is rebuk'd as, it is said,
Mark Antony's was by Caesar. He chid the sisters
When first they put the name of king upon me
And bade them speak to him. Then prophet-like,
They hail'd him father to a line of kings.
Upon my head they plac'd a fruitless crown.
And put a barren sceptre in my gripe,
Thence to be wrench'd with an unlineal hand,
No son of mine succeeding. If't be so,
For Banquo's issue have I fil'd my mind;
For them, the gracious Duncan have I murder'd,
Put rancours in the vessel of my peace
Only for them, and mine eternal jewel
Given to the common enemy of man,
To make them kings, the seed of Banquo kings.
Rather than so, come Fate into the list,
And champion me to th'utterance.

These lines develop his jealousy of his former friend: Banquo might be more royal than he is.

What is the effect of this repetition of 'fear'?

The allusion refers to other rivals – who won?

Who is Macbeth obsessed with here? Look at the pronouns.

What does this collection of words suggest Macbeth is now worried about?

Fil'd means defiled. Why is this very revealing diction?

Why is this a powerful **metaphor**?

Notice the use of the rule of three in 'them' and 'Kings', for rhetorical emphasis.

How does diction reveal Macbeth's sense of guilt?

What is **personified** here? Why choose this imagery?

Tip

Don't forget to make the context point about why Shakespeare wanted to present Banquo as a foil to Macbeth.

Activity 2

The annotated text shows you how to identify features of language, use subject terminology, and explain what it reveals about characters and its effect on audiences.

Explore characters in your own play whose emotions develop or change. For example:

- *Romeo and Juliet*: at the beginning of Act 2 Scene 5, how does love affect the way Juliet expresses herself?

- *Much Ado About Nothing*: at the beginning of Act 2 Scene 3, how does Benedick express his feelings about love and relationships?

- *The Merchant of Venice*: characters don't soliloquize but express their feelings to those they trust. At the beginning of Act 3 Scene 2, how does Portia show Bassanio her feelings for him?

- *Macbeth*: look at Banquo's soliloquy at the beginning of Act 3 Scene 1. How has he changed since Act 2 Scene 1? Is Macbeth right to fear him?

Make notes on their language, making sure you:

- ☑ identify techniques (mark up your copy of the text)
- ☑ quote short examples
- ☑ comment on the effect of language on the audience.

Use the table below to record your findings:

	Parts of speech	Semantic fields	Diction	Reiteration and patterns of repetition	Imagery, e.g. metaphors, similes, personification	Allusions
1.						
2.						
3.						

Write up your findings as a 600-word essay addressing the following question:

> In what ways does Shakespeare's language reveal changing feelings in this extract?

Benedick changes dramatically and comically in Act 2 Scene 3. While Macbeth's changes are tragic, entangling him deeper in the webs woven by the weird sisters, Benedick makes a choice, moving the play towards its comic conclusion. He realizes he actually loves Beatrice. His character is transformed through a relationship.

This is a **prose** soliloquy, showing that although Benedick is high-born, he is a down-to-earth and comic character.

Source text B

Much Ado About Nothing

BENEDICK

Love me? Why, it must be requited. I hear how I am censured. They say I will bear myself proudly if I perceive the love come from her. They say too that she will rather die than give any sign of affection. I did never think to marry. I must not seem proud. Happy are they that hear their detractions and can put them to mending. They say the lady is fair; 'tis a truth, I can bear them witness. And virtuous; 'tis so, I cannot reprove it. And wise, but for loving me. By my troth, it is no addition to her wit nor no great argument of her folly, for I will be horribly in love with her.

Activity 3

As this is prose, explore the **syntax** of Benedick's speech.

1. Find the end of each sentence.

2. How many longer sentences are broken up into short phrases?

3. Read the speech to each other, changing speaker whenever there is a full stop, colon or semi-colon.

4. What makes Benedick's language funny?

5. Find examples, and explain how they show that Benedick is thinking aloud.

Stretch

Compare Benedick's emotions here to those at the beginning of Act 3 Scene 2. How does his language suggest he has changed? Is there evidence that he loved Beatrice all along? Support your response with quotations from both soliloquies.

Key terms

Prose Text written in its ordinary form, without a recognisable structure. In Shakespeare's plays high-status characters usually speak in verse and lower-status characters in prose, but many characters use both. Prose is more frequent in comic scenes; verse dominates in formal or romantic scenes, and in tragedy.

Syntax the structure of a sentence; verse has syntax as well as prose

Tip

Make sure you follow the syntax of verse, just like prose, to appreciate meaning and effects of language.

Relationships

It is important to consider relationships between characters, whichever play you are studying. Love can change our feelings and develop our maturity, just as hate changes Macbeth's relationship with Banquo, and guilt will destroy his relationship with Lady Macbeth.

In this example on page 160, Juliet is waiting for Romeo on her wedding night. Compare Juliet's verse to Benedick's prose. This is an epithalamion, a wedding-night poem. When reading it, consider the various different poetic and linguistic devices Shakespeare uses. What differences are made by the choice of verse or prose at different points in your play?

Source text C

Romeo and Juliet

JULIET

Come, Night, come, Romeo, come, thou day in night,
For thou wilt lie upon the wings of night,
Whiter than new snow on a raven's back.
Come, gentle Night, come, loving, black-brow'd Night,
Give me my Romeo, and, when I shall die,
Take him and cut him out in little stars,
And he will make the face of heaven so fine
That all the world will be in love with night,
And pay no worship to the garish sun.
O, I have bought the mansion of a love,
But not possess'd it, and though I am sold,
Not yet enjoy'd. So tedious is this day
As is the night before some festival
To an impatient child that hath new robes
And may not wear them. O, here comes my Nurse,
And she brings news, and every tongue that speaks
But Romeo's name speaks heavenly eloquence.

She now invokes Romeo as well as the night.

Compare with ways in which Romeo spoke about the night before, when he first met Juliet.

Night becomes a person.

But Romeo becomes the starry sky.

How do these metaphors suggest Juliet's impatience?

Does this image show maturity?

Why does the word 'heavenly' fit what she has said earlier?

Activity 4

Find pictures which can accompany the whole of Juliet's soliloquy. Illustrate the images she paints with her words and connect them to her feelings.

Stretch

Explore the effects of repetition and contrast in Juliet's speech. How do they add urgency and a sense of desire to this scene?

Key term

Imagery: the use of descriptive or figurative language to help a reader visualize an idea

This play takes place over just three days (and nights). How is that pace communicated to the audience here?

This speech presents the powerful effects of **imagery**. Shakespeare's plays are full of references to light and darkness. These are like lighting cues for the audience, as there was no lighting in Shakespeare's theatres. How can light and darkness affect mood? Lovers like the darkness, but so do those with evil intentions.

Activity 5

Explore ways in which language creates a physical setting and mood in your play, looking at the following:

Macbeth: The description of night thickening at the end of Act 3 Scene 2

The Merchant of Venice: Lorenzo and Jessica's duologue at the beginning of Act 5 Scene 1

3

Much Ado About Nothing: The night watch and their arrest of Borrachio and Conrad in Act 3 Scene 3

4

Romeo and Juliet: The description of dawn at the beginning of Act 3 Scene 5

Notice how in each of these the mood of the setting is dramatic, and closely related to characters' feelings.

Activity 6

The language of poetry analysis can be applied to Shakespeare's verse. What do you understand by: rhythm, rhyme, alliteration, assonance and consonance?

1. Define each term and support this by quoting an example.

2. Choose a character from the play you are studying. What is distinctive about his or her verse? Illustrate with reference to *two* different speeches.

Unit 5 Making links and connections

Learning objectives

- To respond in detail to extract-based questions

- To make critical links to other relevant parts of the text

Exam link

AO1 requires you to maintain a critical style and develop an informed personal response.

Answering extract-based questions

Extract-based questions ask you to make links to other parts of the play. How do they do this? Here is an example of an extract-based question:

> Explore the idea that Lorenzo and Jessica represent the possibility of happiness in the play. Refer to this extract from Act 5 Scene 1 and elsewhere in the play.
>
> **[40]**

Begin by highlighting key words in the question. Questions will name one or two characters. Make sure your quote bank is focused on characters and relationships. The question also identifies a topic, which may be controversial. In this example, Lorenzo and Jessica find happiness but at the expense of others. What does the audience think of this?

Source text A

Link to 'In sooth I know not why I am so sad?'

The Merchant of Venice

JESSICA

I am never merry when I hear sweet music.

LORENZO

The reason is your spirits are attentive.
For do but note a wild and wanton herd
Or race of youthful and unhandled colts
Fetching mad bounds, bellowing and neighing loud—
Which is the hot condition of their blood—
If they but hear perchance a trumpet sound,
Or any air of music touch their ears,
You shall perceive them make a mutual stand,
Their savage eyes turn'd to a modest gaze
By the sweet power of music. Therefore the poet
Did feign that Orpheus drew trees, stones and floods;
Since naught so stockish, hard, and full of rage,
But music for the time doth change his nature.
The man that hath no music in himself,
Nor is not mov'd with concord of sweet sounds,
Is fit for treasons, stratagems and spoils;
The motions of his spirit are dull as night
And his affections dark as Erebus.
Let no such man be trusted. Mark the music.

Change of tone/mood in this scene?

Contrast with Lorenzo and Jessica's happiness?

Link to Shylock: beginning of Act 4?

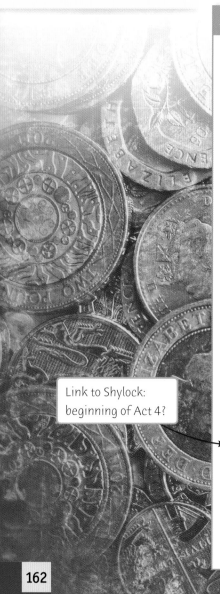

Writing an introduction

The first place to make links is the introduction. Relate the extract to where it fits in the drama, and what it reveals to the audience about characters.

You will thus show your knowledge of the rest of the play by:

- relating characters to the action and issues of the play (AO1)
- exploring the detail of their language (AO2)
- using context to inform your own response (AO3).

Read these example introductions. How successful are they in linking the extract to other parts of the play?

Student A

The extract begins with an allusion to the Roman goddess of hunting and virginity, Diana. The second line has assonance 'sweetest, pierce, ear' which is appropriate for lines about music. Alliteration of 'wild… wanton… bounds… bellowing' and 'blood' suggest the savagery of young animals (or young people) unless charmed by music. The poet alludes to the myth of Orpheus who could tame and charm nature and even the dead with his music. Erebus is a reference to the classical Hell. Thus Lorenzo's metaphors suggest that those who can't respond emotionally to music are the plotters who spoil happiness.

> Overall comments: Textual reference and identification of features of the writing (AO2), but list-like; question is not clearly addressed.

Student B

Lorenzo and Jessica are happy at the end of the play because they have made other characters miserable. Poor Shylock was driven to revenge because they ran off with all his money and his wife's wedding ring and sold it to buy a monkey. Jessica has given up her religion. Shakespeare's world is racist and sexist. Men marry women for their money and expect to live happily ever after. Portia is no better. She has humiliated Shylock and now she is about to play a nasty trick on Bassanio.

> Overall comments: Personal response (AO1) and some understanding of context (AO3). Limited awareness of different audience attitudes/Shakespearean comedy. Lacks focus on extract and quotation.

Student C

Lorenzo and Jessica set the scene in Act 5 Scene 1 for the reconciliation and happiness of the other young couples: Portia with Bassanio and Nerissa with Gratiano. They prepare the audience for the comic conclusion of the play, dramatically changing the atmosphere from the courtroom scenes and the tragedy of Shylock's humiliation. The music and soft lighting and darkness referred to in this scene's imagery are stage direction; they change the atmosphere, and the mood of the audience. The audience knows happiness for Lorenzo and Jessica has come at a price. Lorenzo, like Bassanio, is an impoverished adventurer who has taken a great risk in marrying Jessica. She gave up her family, religion and inheritance. The dramatic irony is that we know Shylock has signed away his money to them: their happiness will come at the price of his grief. Perhaps the lines 'Let no such man be trusted' apply particularly to him.

> Overall comments: Analysis of both extract and question. Extract placed in dramatic and cultural context (AO1).

> Conventions of Shakespearean drama understood (AO3).

> Appreciation of characterization, stagecraft and dramatic irony (AO2).

Exam link

Address all assessment objectives from the beginning of your answer.

Student C's opening paragraph is the strongest as all AOs are addressed. There is no close analysis of language but that belongs in the next paragraph. Do not plunge straight into close reading, but make sure your links and context are relevant to the extract and its dramatic moment in the play. Lorenzo and Jessica are linked to other characters; their happiness is contrasted with Shylock's humiliation.

Close reading of the extract will give you a springboard for more links. Below is an exam-style question with an annotated extract to help you.

> Explore how Romeo's changing emotions influence events in the play. Refer to this extract from Act 5 Scene 1 and elsewhere in the play.
>
> **[40]**

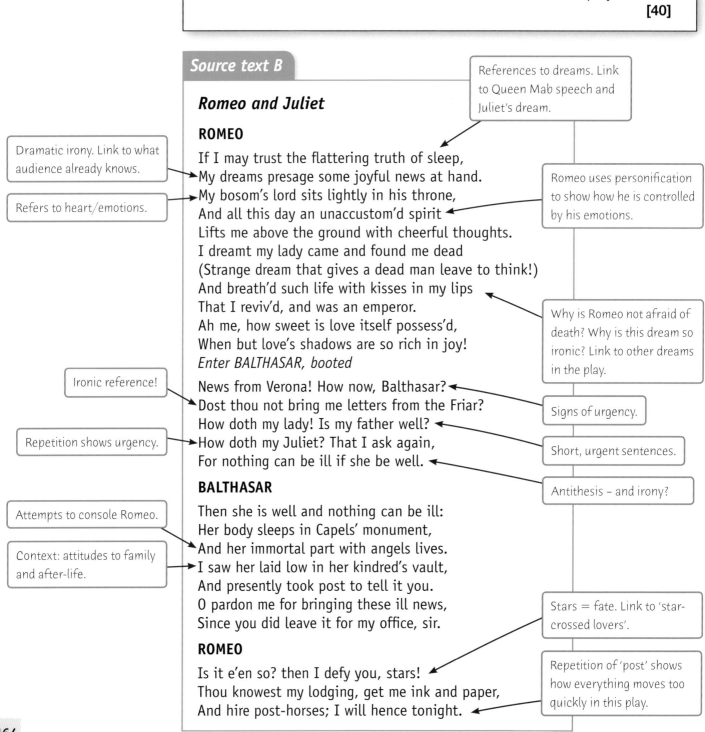

Source text B

Romeo and Juliet

ROMEO

If I may trust the flattering truth of sleep,
My dreams presage some joyful news at hand.
My bosom's lord sits lightly in his throne,
And all this day an unaccustom'd spirit
Lifts me above the ground with cheerful thoughts.
I dreamt my lady came and found me dead
(Strange dream that gives a dead man leave to think!)
And breath'd such life with kisses in my lips
That I reviv'd, and was an emperor.
Ah me, how sweet is love itself possess'd,
When but love's shadows are so rich in joy!
Enter BALTHASAR, booted

News from Verona! How now, Balthasar?
Dost thou not bring me letters from the Friar?
How doth my lady! Is my father well?
How doth my Juliet? That I ask again,
For nothing can be ill if she be well.

BALTHASAR

Then she is well and nothing can be ill:
Her body sleeps in Capels' monument,
And her immortal part with angels lives.
I saw her laid low in her kindred's vault,
And presently took post to tell it you.
O pardon me for bringing these ill news,
Since you did leave it for my office, sir.

ROMEO

Is it e'en so? then I defy you, stars!
Thou knowest my lodging, get me ink and paper,
And hire post-horses; I will hence tonight.

Annotation boxes:
- References to dreams. Link to Queen Mab speech and Juliet's dream.
- Dramatic irony. Link to what audience already knows.
- Refers to heart/emotions.
- Romeo uses personification to show how he is controlled by his emotions.
- Why is Romeo not afraid of death? Why is this dream so ironic? Link to other dreams in the play.
- Ironic reference!
- Repetition shows urgency.
- Signs of urgency.
- Short, urgent sentences.
- Antithesis – and irony?
- Attempts to console Romeo.
- Context: attitudes to family and after-life.
- Stars = fate. Link to 'star-crossed lovers'.
- Repetition of 'post' shows how everything moves too quickly in this play.

The language of this extract has a powerful effect on an audience. Dramatic irony ensures we are aware of the consequences of Romeo's hasty return. Romeo's actions bring on the fatal ending Friar Laurence tried to prevent.

Making links

You should link your close reading to issues, contexts, debates, characters and relationships. Audiences might find Romeo impulsive yet romantic. Or they might find him rash and disturbingly preoccupied with death. The fashion for 'melancholy' in Shakespeare's time might be compared with 'goths' today.

Which view of Romeo does this extract support? This will help you move your essay towards a conclusion.

To answer the question, make links to other parts of the play which also show Romeo's emotional volatility.

Activity 1

Track Romeo's emotions by building a quote bank to show:

- his feelings about Rosaline (end of Act 1 Scene 1)
- how he tells Friar Laurence about Juliet (Act 2 Scene 3)
- his challenge to Tybalt (Act 3 Scene 1)
- his desire to kill himself rather than be banished (Act 3 Scene 3)
- his happiness after the night with Juliet (Act 3 Scene 5): 'come death, and welcome, Juliet wills it so'
- his despair when speaking to the Apothecary (Act 5 Scene 1)
- his violence towards Paris (Act 5 Scene 3)
- his last words.

Use these links to explore the idea that Romeo is preoccupied with death.

Support

Act out the extract opposite with a partner, and try out different ways of performing Romeo's role.

Stretch

1. Find out more about the portrayal of melancholia in Elizabethan art, music and poetry.

2. How might melancholy emotions influence Romeo's choices and fate? How would we regard such emotions today? Is Romeo a dangerous influence on Juliet? Find evidence for this view.

Tip

Support comments on the extract with links to how the character speaks and behaves elsewhere in the play.

165

Tip

Don't be afraid to say what you think, or to use the word 'I'. Show you appreciate different interpretations of a character or relationship. Then give your own *personal response*, supported by evidence. Examiners are not looking for a single 'right answer'.

Activity 2

Use extracts to review your reactions to a character, remembering different audiences could view him or her in different ways.

1. Choose an extract which shows how audiences are intended to judge characters and relationships. Look at the last act of your play, for example:

   - *Macbeth*: Malcolm's closing words about Macbeth and Lady Macbeth
   - *Macbeth*: Macbeth's reaction to Lady Macbeth's death
   - *Romeo and Juliet*: Juliet's reaction to Romeo's death
   - *Much Ado About Nothing*: Benedick's reaction when Don Pedro taunts him as 'the married man'
   - *The Merchant of Venice*: how Antonio pledges his soul that Bassanio will be loyal to Portia.

2. To what extent do these final words settle audiences' arguments about these complex characters and relationships?

3. Link the passage to earlier scenes from your quote bank as support for your own view.

The extract you are given in the exam is chosen to help you make links to other parts of the play.

Activity 3

Choose an extract about 30 lines long, which you have found in the final scene of your studied play. Match it to the question below, and use it as a springboard to explore issues in the play.

Explore how successful Friar Laurence is in justifying his actions in the final scene and elsewhere in the play.

[40]

Explore the ways in which Gratiano and Nerissa contribute to the comedy of *The Merchant of Venice* in the final scene and elsewhere in the play.

[40]

Explore the extent to which an audience can feel pity for Lady Macbeth.

[40]

Explore how convincing you find the relationship of Hero and Claudio in the final scene and elsewhere in the play.

[40]

Activity 4

1. Now choose a short scene from *anywhere* in your play and write an extract-based question. It will need to:

   - focus on a single character or relationship
   - be a dramatic and interesting moment from the play
   - illustrate a key topic or issue in the play
   - allow you to make links to other scenes.

2. Share your question with others. Revise it until it tests all the AOs.

3. Then write an answer which:

   - makes an argued response to the question
   - considers the significance of context
   - looks in detail at language
   - makes links to other scenes involving the same characters and ideas
   - uses your quote bank to support your answer
   - presents a personal conclusion based on evaluating the evidence.

Unit 6 Getting ready for the exam

Learning objectives

- To plan answers to whole-text questions
- To ensure the assessment objectives are addressed
- To structure and check responses

Tip

Use this mnemonic to remember the points to focus on in your response:

- **CH**aracters
- **A**nalysis
- **R**elationships
- **T**opics

Key terms

Effects the impact the writer has on the reader/audience through language, structure, imagery or sound effects

Affect to have an impact on the reader or audience emotionally

The exam question

In the exam you will have a choice of two questions:

1. Either write about the extract, making short links and connections to other parts of the play.

2. Explore at least two moments from the play to answer an essay question.

You will be assessed on both questions as follows:

Assessment Objective		% of marks
A01:	*Critical interpretation* and textual support	35%
A02:	Language *analysis*	35%
A03:	Understanding of context	20%
A04:	Vocabulary, sentences, spelling and punctuation	10%

In this question, 4 marks will be awarded for A04: use of a range of vocabulary and sentence structures for clarity, purpose and effect with accurate spelling and punctuation.

When you choose your own moments from the play, make sure they help you to:

Address the question, showing knowledge of the play	A01
Explore the dramatist's **effects** through analysis of language and form	A02
Understand how Shakespeare's writing **affects** the audience's emotions	A02
Appreciate how context can influence different responses	A03
Conclude your personal response	A01

Planning your response

You have 45 minutes to write your response so you will not be able to cover everything. Aim to cover the following:

- an *introduction* opening out implications in the question
- detailed *exploration* of three key moments from different parts of the play (or two key moments looking at different interpretations/contexts, introduced by 'however')
- a *conclusion* giving your personal response, based on your evidence.

Allowing time for planning and checking, you have only about 8 minutes for each paragraph. Make sure you have specific things to say about each key moment to gain marks.

The tragedies: a journey to destruction

Activity 1

The journey for tragic characters is a road to death and disaster. Draw a 'road map' table for each tragic character. Here's an example for Macbeth:

Stage of journey	Topics to explore	Specific scenes and quotations
Initial problems	When Macbeth meets the weird sisters they appeal to his ambition.	Act 1 Scene 3 'Why do I yield to that suggestion...' Beginning Act 1 scene 4: 'Stars hide your fires...'
Wrong choices	He is persuaded by Lady Macbeth to go against his better judgement.	Act 1 Scene 7 'I dare do all that may become a man...' 'Bring forth men-children only...'
Influence of fate or fortune	When he goes back to the sisters, his frustration leads to further murders.	Act 4 Scene 1 'From this moment,/ The very firstlings of my heart shall be/The firstlings of my hand...'
Response of audience	We are appalled by what Macbeth has become, but admire his self-knowledge and bravery in defiance of his fate.	Act 5 Scene 3 'I have lived long enough...' Act 5 Scene 5 'Life's but a walking shadow...'

Tip

Don't learn short quotations from all over the play. Concentrate on key moments for each character and learn two or three quotations from them, so that you can comment in detail on their language and effects.

Characters in relationships

Relationships can contribute to tragedy, as they influence the choices characters make.

In comedies, characters who form successful and happy relationships end up overcoming their problems: Shakespearean comedies therefore end in marriages. Characters outside the pattern of happy relationships cause many of the problems which arise.

Here is an example of an essay question.

Activity 2

1. Divide characters in your play into *couples* and *outsiders*.
2. How have relationships, or the lack of a relationship, influenced the ways in which the play has developed?
3. Which characters have changed relationships or changed category?
4. How does Shakespeare's language show relationships improving or worsening?
5. Which key scenes illustrate relationships?
6. Discuss with a partner. Have you come to the same conclusions?

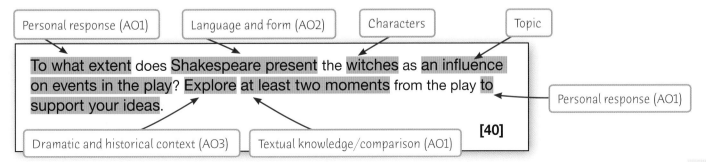

Personal response (AO1)   Language and form (AO2)   Characters   Topic

To what extent does Shakespeare present the witches as an influence on events in the play? Explore at least two moments from the play to support your ideas.

Personal response (AO1)

Dramatic and historical context (AO3)   Textual knowledge/comparison (AO1)

[40]

Preparing topics

Unlike the extract-based task, which has the instruction to 'explore', the whole-text task asks a specific question. Key phrases encourage you to explore and debate about characters. For example:

Activity 3

1. Read the exam-style questions on page 169 and below. Use the table on page 168 to identify what they are asking.

> In what ways does Shakespeare's portrayal of Lord and Lady Capulet explain the choices Juliet makes? Explore at least two moments from the play to support your ideas.
>
> [40]

> In what ways does Shakespeare show Portia taking control of the action of the play? Explore at least two moments from the play to support your ideas.
>
> [40]

> How and why do you think Shakespeare presents such a dramatic change in Benedick's attitude to women? Explore at least two moments from the play to support your ideas.
>
> [40]

2. Choose the question on your play. Which moments in the play would you write about? Make a note of these.

Writing an introduction to the whole-text question

It is important to begin well. Do not answer the question yet (save that for your conclusion). Try to open out its implications by:

- addressing all three AOs in your first paragraph

- giving an overview of the whole play and the characters, relationships and issues mentioned in the question

- introducing your key moments and their significance.

Think about that first paragraph carefully. Spelling and punctuation must make a good impression. All these students have made a good start, but some are better than others.

Student A

'Fair is foul and foul is fair': the witches' chant at the end of the first scene is memorably alliterative and antithetical announcing a world where morality is upside-down. Shakespeare makes the audience suspicious when Macbeth announces 'so foul and fair a day I have not seen'. The witches certainly influence the language of the play; do they really influence its action? The weird sisters tell Macbeth the future, but he makes his own choices. He sees the witches just twice, once involuntarily, before deciding to kill Duncan, and then by choice, before ordering the slaughter of Macduff's family.

> Quotation – an unusual but striking way to begin (AO1).

> Analysis of witches' verses referencing terminology (AO2) and context (AO3).

> Detailed knowledge (AO1) and critical debate.

> Chooses key scenes.

Student B

Benedick is the most comic characters in the play, contrasting with Claudio and Don Pedro who are more serious. The audience enjoy his banter even if his attitudes are sexist today. He learns his lesson and completely changes his view of Beatrice. I think he always liked her really and it was a kind of love-hate realationship. Shakespear suggests love and hate are two sides of the same coin. Two scenes showing Beneidick's attitudes are when he tells Don Pedro he 'cannot endure Lady Tongue', as this gives Don Pedro the idea of the practical joke. Later he says 'he will be horribly in love with her. It's a dramatic and amusing change.

> Understands Benedick's comic role (AO2).

> Appreciates context (AO3).

> Personal response and textual knowledge (AO1).

> Chooses key scenes and shows personal response.

Student C

Lord and Lady capulet are juliets parents. They are very harsh. Lady Capulet does not even know julies birthday and wants to marry her off to Paris as quick as possible, although she is only 13. Capulet wants her married to paris so as to get back in with the Prince after the fight. Juliet has like no say in this. It aint surprising that she prefers Romeo and keeps secrets from em cos she could never tell em the truth. I'm gonna look when her mum tells her to marry, and when her dad sez hell drag her to church if she dont.

> Understands the plot of the play (AO1).

> Chooses two key moments.

> Lacks reference to the writer, the drama, its language or the context.

Student D

Portia is supposed to marry the man her father has chosen through the casket test but obviously has her own opinions and she really fancies Bassanio so she is happy when the others fail the test and she gets to marry him but he has a real problem because of the 'bond' that Antonio has with Shylock and she sorts this out by dressing up as a young man so takes charge like.

> Narrating story, not analysing.

> References to 'bond' and Portia at court more promising.

How you write matters, as well as *what* you write. Use ambitious vocabulary and vary your sentences for effect. Simple sentences can make strong points very effectively. Use longer sentences for more complex points, such as balancing one viewpoint about a text with another.

Addressing AO4

Shakespeare essays are marked out of 40: up to 36 marks are available for AO1, AO2 and AO3, and 4 marks are available for AO4, spelling, punctuation and grammar.

> **Activity 4**
>
> Student A uses a wide variety of sentence types and punctuation to organize their answer. Rewrite the other answers to gain more marks for AO4. Student B has problems with spelling, Student D with punctuation and Student C's essay is too informal.

Writing conclusions

When revising, practise opening paragraphs and selecting scenes. You should also practise conclusions. Look at these examples:

Student E

The witches are the most scary and interesting part of the play and it is a shame they don't come back at the end like they do in the film.

> Aware that the Polanski film ends differently, but does not answer the question.

Student F

Benedick is transformed from someone who seems to hate women and marriage into someone who will defend them even when the other men (including Hero's own father) turn against him. The key to this is the influence of Beatrice. He seems to enjoy the way she challenges him and even makes him more poetic. For the audience, the change in Benedick is the funniest part of the play, and helps the play towards its happy ending.

> Relates Benedick to other men in the play.

> Understanding of comic genre.

> Stronger personal response and awareness of critical debate needed for higher marks.

Student G

Pressure to marry from Lady Capulet and Capulet only makes Juliet more rebellious. Her modern attitudes make her an appealing teenage heroine. Capulet's violent language drives her towards the 'fake suicide' and its fatal consequences for Romeo as well as herself, so he carries a lot of the blame for the tragedy. The Nurse and other adults in the play also seem afraid to confront him, so in my view it is not surprising that Juliet keeps her marriage a secret and only trusts Friar Laurence. It is ironic that Verona only has peace once the young people in the play have nearly all been killed.

> Informed personal response.

> Critical view based on evaluating the evidence.

Student H

Thus Portia not only controls the casket game to make sure the best man wins, but finds a solution in the courtroom which gets Bassanio and all his friends out of trouble, and, through the ring trick, reveals all she has done and embarrasses Bassanio. Shakespeare makes her and Belmont the winners in the end, even though some in a modern audience will feel that the tragedy of Shylock's downfall and humiliation by the laws of Venice is more powerful than the comic happy ending.

> Good textual knowledge and choice of examples.

> Awareness of other ways of reacting to the text.

> Sensitive to the writer's craft and its effect in the theatre.

Don't be afraid of expressing your own opinions, but back them up!

Progress check

Now you have reached the end of the chapter you should be gaining confidence in your understanding of Shakespearean texts, and how to talk about them in the exam. Use the questions below to check your knowledge and understanding.

	I still have some questions about this	I am sure I understand this	I am confident I can give clear explanations with examples
I understand differences between Shakespearean and modern drama.			
I appreciate poetic effects in Shakespeare's writing.			
I understand tragedy and comedy.			
I appreciate dramatic irony.			
I can explain some of the language and allusions.			
I can see why Shakespeare's subjects are still important today.			
I can analyse the effect of imagery and how it affects the audience.			
I understand why different audiences react differently to characters and issues.			
I can confidently express and support my personal response.			
I write in a critical style, and use a range of vocabulary and sentence structures accurately.			

Glossary

Active reading - reading something to understand and evaluate it for its relevance to your needs, for example, underlining key phrases that relate to the exam question

Affect - to have an impact on the reader or audience emotionally

Allusion - a reference to another text, legend or historical event for the purpose of comparison

Anaphora - the repetition of a word or phrase at the beginning of successive clauses

Archaic language - words that are no longer used in everyday language and have lost a particular meaning

Atmosphere - a feeling or tone created by imagery and language

'At-rise' description - how the stage looks when the curtain rises at the beginning of an act or a scene in a play

Ballad - a form of verse or narrative, often set to music

Bathos - when an outcome is so unexpected or disappointing that it becomes comical

Chronological - actions in the order of which they happened

Chronology - the sequence of events in which they first occurred

Comedy - a play that provokes an audience to laugh, which has a happy ending with characters reconciled or even married

Complex sentence - a sentence containing a subordinate clause or clauses

Compound sentence - linking two simple sentences by a connective, for example: *and, but, however*

Connotation - the secondary or associated meaning of a word in addition to its literal meaning

Context - the setting or circumstances of when a text was written

Declarative sentence - a sentence that states a fact

Development - the way a character or text moves on and changes, showing different dimensions

Diction - the choice of words, which thus creates the tone of a character's voice and affects the mood of the scene

Didactic - when a play, novel or speech teaches a specific lesson

Discourse marker - words like *anyway, so, okay* that help organize speech or text

Dramatic irony - when the audience is aware of something inevitable that is about to happen, unknown to the characters

Effects - the impact the writer has on the reader/audience through language, structure, imagery or sound effects

Empathy - our ability to relate to the emotions of someone else

End-stopping - use of punctuation at the end of a line

Enjambment - a run-on line with no punctuation, which should be read without pausing

Figurative language - language used to describe by comparing it to something else, using words not to be taken literally, such as in metaphors and similes

Foil - a contrasting character who brings out opposite qualities to his or her counterpart, for example, Banquo's conscience contrasts with Macbeth's ambition

Formal language - language that has strict grammatical structures and generally uses standard or technical vocabulary

Genre - the form of a literary text, such as a tragedy or comedy

Gothic - a genre of fiction that is designed to unsettle; one of its features is old buildings with secret passageways, winding staircases and narrow hallways

Iambic pentameter - the five-beat line made up of unstressed and stressed syllables which Shakespeare uses most frequently in his plays; when unrhymed, this is called blank verse

Imagery - the use of descriptive or figurative language to help a reader visualise an idea

Imperative - expressing a command

Infer - to conclude a meaning which is not explicitly stated

Irony - when the surface meaning is opposite to the intended meaning, like sarcasm, but when nobody is insulted

Main clause - a clause that can stand alone as a sentence

Metaphor - when a writer describes something as if it is something else

Narrative - an account of events; a story

Nuance - a finer, less obvious detail

Oxymoron - a combination of words that have opposite or contradictory meanings, such as the phrase bitter sweet

Pathetic fallacy - when an author attributes human emotions to aspects of nature, such as 'an angry storm' or 'sullen rocks'

Pathos - a feeling of sympathy or compassion or pity

Personification - when a writer gives an inhuman thing human qualities, for example, 'the tree waived its arms in the wind'

Prose - In Shakespeare's plays high-status characters usually speak in verse and lower-status characters in prose, but many characters use both. Prose is more frequent in comic scenes; verse dominates in formal or romantic scenes, and in tragedy.

Quatrain - a four-line section of verse

Register - a particular style of language, which varies according to its purpose,

Reiteration - repeating the same word or action

Rhyming couplet - a pair of lines in which the final stressed syllables rhyme

Satire - when an important person or organization is made fun of

Semantic field - a group of words related to the same subject, therefore creating a detailed description

Setting - the location of events

Simile - when a writer describes something as if it is like something else.

Soliloquy - when a character speaks to the audience and tells us their true thoughts, usually because they are keeping a secret or can't make up their minds about something

Stanza - a group of lines forming the basic recurring unit in a poem; a verse

Structure - how a piece of writing is put together; how the choices of language, punctuation and form affect the message or meaning being conveyed

Subordinate clause - the part of a sentence, which is dependent on the main clause for its meaning, and cannot stand on its own

Symbol - An object or sign which represents something else. This can be especially true of something physical representing something abstract. For instance, the symbol of justice is a pair of weighing scales.

Synonym - a word or phrase that has the same meaning as another word or phrase

Syntax - the structure of a sentence structure for example, verse has syntax, as well as prose

Theme - a subject or idea that is explored in a literary work

Tone - how the attitude of a character or writer is portrayed in the language, for example, Inspector Goole's tone is authoritative; Meera Syal's tone in Anita and Me is comic

Tragedy - a play that stimulates pity and fear in the audience, as it shows the characters the mercy of fate

Tricolon - repeating a word or phrase three times

Verisimilitude - a realistic, lifelike or natural quality to language, such as when sensory language, connected with sight, sound or smell, creates verisimilitude

Acknowledgements

The authors and publisher are grateful for permission to reprint extracts from the following copyright material:

Simon Armitage: 'Homecoming' from *Cloud Cuckoo Land* (Faber, 2004), copyright © Simon Armitage 2004, reprinted by permission of Faber & Faber Ltd.

J G Ballard: opening of 'Passport to Eternity', copyright © J G Ballard 1962, from *Passport to Eternity* (Berkley, 1963), reprinted by permission of the Wylie Agency (UK) Ltd for the Estate of J G Ballard.

Gillian Clarke: lines from 'Lament' and from 'Cold Knap Lake' from *Collected Poems* (Carcanet, 1997), reprinted by permission of Carcanet Press Ltd.

Carol Ann Duffy: 'In Mrs Tilscher's Class' from *The Other Country* (Anvil, 1990), copyright © Carol Ann Duffy 1990, and lines from 'Warming Her Pearls' from *Selling Manhattan* (Anvil, 1987), copyright © Carol Ann Duffy 1987, reprinted by permission of the author c/o Rogers, Coleridge & White Ltd, 20 Powis Mews, London W11 1JN

Thom Gunn: lines from 'Baby Song' from *Collected Poems* (Faber, 1993), reprinted by permission of Faber & Faber Ltd.

Seamus Heaney: 'Digging' from *Death of a Naturalist* (Faber, 1966) , copyright © Seamus Heaney 1966, reprinted by permission of Faber & Faber Ltd.

Nick Hornby: extract from *About a Boy* (Penguin, 2000), copyright © Nick Hornby 2000, reprinted by permission of Penguin Books Ltd.

Langston Hughes: lines from 'Dreams' in *The Collected Poems of Langston Hughes* (Vintage, 1995), reprinted by permission of David Higham Associates.

Kazuo Ishiguro: extract from *Never Let Me Go* (Faber, 2005), copyright © Kazuo Ishiguro 2005, reprinted by permission of Faber & Faber Ltd.

Charlotte Keatley: extract from *My Mother Said I Never Should* (Methuen Drama, 1990), copyright © Charlotte Keatley 1990, reprinted by permission of Bloomsbury Methuen Drama, an imprint of Bloomsbury Publishing Plc.

Philip Larkin: lines from 'An Arundel Tomb' from *The Complete Poems* (Faber, 2012), reprinted by permission of Faber & Faber Ltd.

Mike Leigh: extract from *Grief* (Faber, 2011), copyright © Mike Leigh 2011, reprinted by permission of Faber & Faber Ltd.

Simon Stephens: extract from *Punk Rock* (Methuen Drama, 2009), copyright © Simon Stephens 2009, reprinted by permission of Bloomsbury Methuen Drama, an imprint of Bloomsbury Publishing Plc.

Meera Syal: extract from *Anita and Me* (Harper Perennial, 2004), copyright © Meera Syal 1986, reprinted by permission of HarperCollins Publishers Ltd.

Urban Dictionary: definitions from www.urbandictionary.com reprinted by permission of Urban Dictionary.

Derek Walcott: lines from 'Love after Love' from *Collected Poems 1948-1984* (Faber, 1992), copyright © Derek Walcott 1986, reprinted by permission of Faber & Faber Ltd.

Although we have made every effort to trace and contact all copyright holders before publication this has not been possible in all cases. If notified, the publisher will rectify any errors or omissions at the earliest opportunity.

The authors and publisher would like to thank the following for permissions to use their photographs:

Cover: DrAfter123/Getty Images

p12-13: Donald Cooper/photostage.co.uk; **p14:** theatrepix/Alamy Stock Photo; **p15:** ZUMA Press, Inc./Alamy Stock Photo; **p16:** Beatricee/Shutterstock; **p17:** Donald Cooper/photostage.co.uk; **p18:** Q2A Media; **p21:** StudioSmart/Shutterstock; **p20:** ZUMA Press, Inc./Alamy Stock Photo; **p23:** Moviestore collection Ltd/Alamy Stock Photo; **p24:** AF archive/Alamy Stock Photo; **p25:** AF archive/Alamy Stock Photo; **p26:** ShaunWilkinson/Shutterstock; **p27:** Johner Images/Alamy Stock Photo; **p28:** Mary Evans Picture Library; **p29:** Tommaso Sparnacci/Alamy Stock Photo; **p30:** AF archive/Alamy Stock Photo; **p31:** Donald Cooper/photostage.co.uk; **p33:** AF archive/Alamy Stock Photo; **p35:** Joyce Vincent/Shutterstock; **p36:** AF archive/Alamy Stock Photo; **p37:** ZUMA Press, Inc./Alamy Stock Photo; **p42:** Donald Cooper/photostage.co.uk; **p44:** incamerastock/Alamy Stock Photo; **p48-49:** AF archive/Alamy Stock Photo; **p51:** Adam Burton/Alamy Stock Photo; **p50:** WILDLIFE GmbH/Alamy Stock Photo; **p52-53:** MasPix/ Alamy Stock Photo; **p54:** AF archive/Alamy Stock Photo; **p56:** Pictorial Press Ltd/Alamy Stock Photo; **p59:** Ian Dagnall/Alamy Stock Photo; **p60:** Pictorial Press Ltd/Alamy Stock Photo; **p63:** Everett Collection/ REX/Shutterstock; **p65:** ZUMA Press, Inc./Alamy Stock Photo; **p66:** AF archive/Alamy Stock Photo; **p68:** AF archive/Alamy Stock Photo; **p69:** AF archive/Alamy Stock Photo; **p71:** Pictorial Press Ltd/Alamy Stock Photo; **p73:** Photos 12/Alamy Stock Photo; **p74:** Mary Evans Picture Library/Alamy Stock Photo; **p77:** Mary Evans Picture Library/Alamy Stock Photo; **p78:** AF archive/Alamy Stock Photo; **p79:** Photos 12/Alamy Stock Photo; **p80:** Kurt Hutton/Picture Post/Getty Images; **p81:** AF archive/Alamy Stock Photo; **p84:** AF archive/Alamy Stock Photo; **p85:** AF archive/Alamy Stock Photo; **p86:** Oliver Burston/Alamy Stock Photo; **p88-89:** Jenny Sturm/Shutterstock; **p91:** Mary Evans Picture Library/Alamy Stock Photo; **p93:** Hannamariah/Shutterstock; **p94:** savitskaya iryna/Shutterstock; Christin Lola/Shutterstock; Halfpoint/Shutterstock; OJO Images Ltd/Alamy Stock Photo; **p97:** pinkomelet/Shutterstock; **p99:** JEVGENIJA/Alamy Stock Photo; **p100:** Anettphoto/Shutterstock; **p101:** Oleg Zabielin/Shutterstock; **p103:** Pavelk/Shutterstock; **p104:** arbit/Shutterstock; **p105:** Jenny Sturm/Shutterstock; **p106:** mangostock/Shutterstock; **p109:** Outdoor-Archiv/Alamy Stock Photo; **p110:** LiliGraphie/Shutterstock; **p112:** RF Corbis Value/Alamy Stock Photo; **p115:** solarseven/Shutterstock; **p117:** Brent Beach/Alamy Stock Photo; **p118-119:** Mode Image /Alamy Stock Photo; **p121:** Ta da!/Alamy Stock Photo; **p122:** yoshi0511/shutterstock; **p124:** GL Portrait/Alamy Stock Photo; **p126-127:** Priadilshchikova Natalia; **p130:** Sean Pavone/Alamy Stock Photo; **p132-133:** Donald Cooper/photostage.co.uk; **p134:** SPUTNIK/Alamy Stock Photo; **p136:** padu_foto/shutterstock; **p137:** Pictorial Press Ltd/Alamy Stock Photo; **p138:** World History Archive/Alamy Stock Photo; **p139:** AF archive/ Alamy Stock Photo; **p140:** AF archive/Alamy Stock Photo; **p142:** Moviestore collection Ltd/Alamy Stock Photo; **p143:** Robbie Jack/Corbis; **p147:** Franz-Marc Frei/Corbis; **p148:** AF archive/Alamy Stock Photo; **p146:** AF archive/Alamy Stock Photo; **p149:** sjtheatre/Alamy Stock Photo; sjtheatre/Alamy Stock Photo; **p150:** Donald Cooper/photostage.co.uk; **p152:** AF archive/Alamy Stock Photo; **p155:** archive/Alamy Stock Photo; **p156:** Moviestore collection Ltd/Alamy Stock Photo; **p158:** Moviestore collection Ltd/Alamy Stock Photo; **p160:** AF archive/Alamy Stock Photo; **p162:** EYESITE/Stockimo/Alamy Stock Photo; **p165:** Moviestore collection Ltd/Alamy Stock Photo; **p166:** Chris H.D. Davis/Alamy Stock Photo.

Page layout by Aptara.